1 2 P9-CTA-674 7 8 ★

★ 3

14 4 5 6 9

10

15 13 12 11 ★

16 23

19 20 ★

17 22 24

18 21

★

Green Christmas

Eilidh Gallagher (whose name is pronounced like Hayley, without the H) is an award-winning sustainability blogger, vlogger and freelance writer. She lives in Bedford, UK with her fiancé and three children.

BLOOMSBURY PUBLISHING
Bloomsbury Publishing Plc
50 Bedford Square, London, WC1B 3DP, UK

BLOOMSBURY, BLOOMSBURY PUBLISHING and the Diana logo are trademarks of Bloomsbury Publishing Plc

First published in Great Britain 2020

A catalogue record for this book is available from the British Library

Library of Congress Cataloguing-in-Publication data has been applied for

ISBN: HB: 978-1-5266-2834-3; eBook: 978-1-5266-2835-0

10 9 8 7 6 5 4 3 2 1

Editor: Xa Shaw Stewart
Project Editor: Sophie Elletson
Designer: Emily Voller
Illustrator: Holly Ovenden

Printed and bound in China by C&C Offset Printing co. Ltd

MIX
Paper from responsible sources
FSC® C008047

This book is printed using inks made from soybeans. Compared to traditional petroleum-based ink, soy-based ink is accepted as more environmentally friendly. Soy inks show good rub resistance, have good stability on press and give clear bright colours and make it easier to recycle paper.

To find out more about our authors and books visit www.bloomsbury.com and sign up for our newsletters

EILIDH GALLAGHER

Green Christmas

Little changes that bring joy & help the planet

BLOOMSBURY PUBLISHING

LONDON • OXFORD • NEW YORK • NEW DELHI • SYDNEY

Choosing a
Green Christmas

Two million turkeys, 74 million mince pies, 17.2 million Brussels sprouts and 227,000 miles of wrapping paper. No, this isn't the amount we *buy* at Christmas time, but the huge amount that is thrown out and wasted.

It's hard not to feel even a little guilty about the sheer excess of a modern Christmas and the effect it has on our planet. Christmas is meant to be about so much more than just 'stuff' and yet we all end up feeling the pressure to keep up with expectations, to make each Christmas bigger and better than the last, to spend, spend, spend.

Maybe you've been looking for the opportunity to start making greener choices. Perhaps you are tired of the stress that seems to start building from October. Or perhaps you simply want a Christmas focused on more than just the presents.

Whatever your reasons, there are so many different ways to have a greener Christmas without compromising on the fun. This book will give you plenty of ideas in 24 Christmassy chapters.

If you are just starting out on your path to a greener Christmas, don't try to do everything at once. It's much better to pick one or two areas to focus on and add more each year, than trying to make too many changes and failing to do any!

Being green is all about the journey.

Contents

Slow
Christmas

The run-up to Christmas can be frantic, with food to prepare, presents to buy and family to host. Sometimes it is easy to lose sight of what makes Christmas so special. This year take a breath, slow down and think about how the festive season can inspire you to lead a greener, more meaningful life all year round.

What Does Christmas Mean to You?

This simple exercise can help you focus on the things that really matter to you at Christmas.

1 Write down your favourite Christmas memories on the next page, which I've left blank for you.

2 Think about the five senses and connect them to your Christmas experiences. Do you have a favourite Christmas smell, foods you love or a special song that never fails to make you smile?

3 Which activities do you especially enjoy during the festive season?

4 What don't you like about Christmas? What would you like to avoid if you could?

Now you have the ingredients to create the most magical Christmas for YOU! Some of your answers will be simple and others more extravagant, but they will all be special. You can always come back to these lists and keep adding to them.

Encourage other adults you live with to do this exercise too and compare your answers. If they are wildly different it's a good opportunity to discuss how you could try to meet in the middle in a way that makes you all happy.

....
....
....
....
....
....
....
....
....
....
....
....
....
....
....
....
....
....
....

Comparison is the thief of joy . . .

If I had asked you to tell me your perfect Christmas before doing that exercise, you might have described those glittery, picture-perfect images that we're bombarded with in ads and on social media. These can lead to a sense that you need to pull out all the stops and achieve that same level of perfection – even if you'd really prefer it to be much more simple, and greener.

Of course we all want Christmas to be magical and special. But slowing down and looking at the big picture can help you to enjoy the whole of the festive season without the stress of trying to keep up with expectations; it also means you have the chance to think about more sustainable choices that you might want to make.

If you can manage to let go of that search for perfection, you will find it much easier to relax and appreciate the moment. So think about what works for you and don't get hung up on the little things that don't go to plan!

Embracing the Season

Celebrating the whole of the winter season and embracing all that December has to offer gives you the opportunity to reconnect with the natural world, as well as taking the pressure off Christmas Day itself.

Take time to soak up the quieter pockets of joy that are unique to this time of year: foraging for decorations, sitting in front of a fire or getting cosy with blankets and a shared story.

Marking the winter solstice can be a wonderful way to celebrate togetherness at Christmas time if not everyone in your family shares the same beliefs. Winter solstice is the shortest day and longest night of the year, and it usually falls on a date around 21 December. Many celebrations in the northern hemisphere focus on this sacred time, as it's when the promise of light and life returns to the natural world. From here, the nights get shorter and the days grow longer until the summer solstice – the longest day and shortest night – in June.

To honour the winter solstice and nature's cycles, you could:

- Make a modern-day yule tree by decorating a living tree outside with food for the animals. Homemade bird feeders and garlands made of popcorn (see Popcorn Strings on page 112) make lovely solstice tree decorations.

- Make your own winter solstice lantern. Or attend a local solstice lantern event (have a look for these online).

- Read winter solstice books and stories together. It's also a great time to learn more about the seasons with the kids.

- Enjoy the darkest night of the year by candlelight – perhaps invite friends and family over for a candlelit feast! You could serve a yule log cake, inspired by the special log that was traditionally burned on the night of winter solstice.

Festive Planning

I will let you in on a secret: planning early makes such a difference. I used to find Christmas stressful because I wanted to do so many things but hadn't allowed any time for planning when they would actually happen, or when I would find the things I needed to make them happen, or how I was going to afford all the things at the same time. Phew! No wonder I was feeling stressed.

Planning early means you can relax and enjoy a Christmas that is both sustainable and magical.

Using a Planner

In the months leading up to Christmas, start thinking ahead about everything you want to do in December, whether it's going to see Santa or arranging a festive meal with friends. Draw it out on a big piece of paper, write a list, use a diary or download an app. Just try to keep everything in one place.

If you have kids, as soon as you get dates through for performances, parties and all the other Christmas events, put them on your planner.

Do you do your Christmas food shop online? Then get your order in as soon as the delivery slots are up for grabs. You can update it over the coming weeks, but at least you know you've got a slot.

If you order your turkey from the butcher or veg box from a local supplier, check when you will need to do that and mark it on the planner too.

Christmas activities

Each year, I create a plan of December and place an activity or outing on a different day. Obviously things can change, so I think of it as more of a wish list. If we get to do it all, great, but I try not to feel like we absolutely *have to* do it all. Popular activities, such as visiting Santa, can get booked up early, sometimes even before the end of October, so make sure you don't leave it too late.

Don't pack too much in, as it will just cause you to feel overwhelmed and you won't enjoy everything nice you have planned. Try to make sure you have factored in some time to just be together (see the Being Together chapter on page 125).

Who are you going to spend Christmas with?

Remember that you can decide to do whatever will make you happiest this Christmas and perhaps that means spending the day with a friend, or just your immediate family. It's up to you. Catch up with family members or friends well in advance in order to make sure you see everyone you want to see – and to spread out the Christmas chaos!

Making a Gift List

Write a list of all the people you want to buy or make gifts for, then begin thinking about what they might like, or ask them directly. If you want to cut down on the number of gifts this year, check out the ideas in The Giving of Gifts chapter (see page 31). You'll also find some tips for how to approach this tricky conversation with family and friends.

If you plan to make homemade gifts and/or forage for items, think about what you'll need as early as possible. A lot of fruits and leaves are at their most abundant in the autumn. Start saving jars to store your homemade sloe gin, jams and chutneys. Make sure you leave enough time to complete everything before December rolls around.

Budgeting

There are so many lovely things you can do in the run-up to Christmas without spending more than you have. Remember that of all the things you want from Christmas, getting into debt probably isn't one of them.

It's up to you whether you set a ballpark figure or a strict one. Maybe you have saved money into a separate account throughout the year and know exactly how much you have to spend.

Having a budget and a plan will help you stay grounded and not get sucked into a shopping frenzy! Start looking for free local events and adding them to your planner.

Getting Organised

Before buying anything new, check what Christmas decorations, gifts, wrapping paper and other essentials you already have.

Make a note of items you'll need to replace or that you want to get this year. Do this in November so that you have time to source eco-friendly items and look through your local charity shops. Selling sites like Gumtree and Freecycle, as well as your local selling pages and Marketplace on Facebook, are all great places too.

Now is also the time to start looking for pieces of fabric if you are planning on wrapping your gifts with fabric this year.

If you are hosting Christmas or throwing a party, check if you will need to buy things like glasses, cutlery or plates. This will allow you time to source them carefully, rather than falling into the trap of panic-buying things that you don't really need.

The run-up to Christmas is a great time to declutter. Anything that you no longer want or need, you could either sell, offer to local friends and family or donate. If you do this before December, not only will your house be free from clutter, other people will benefit too!

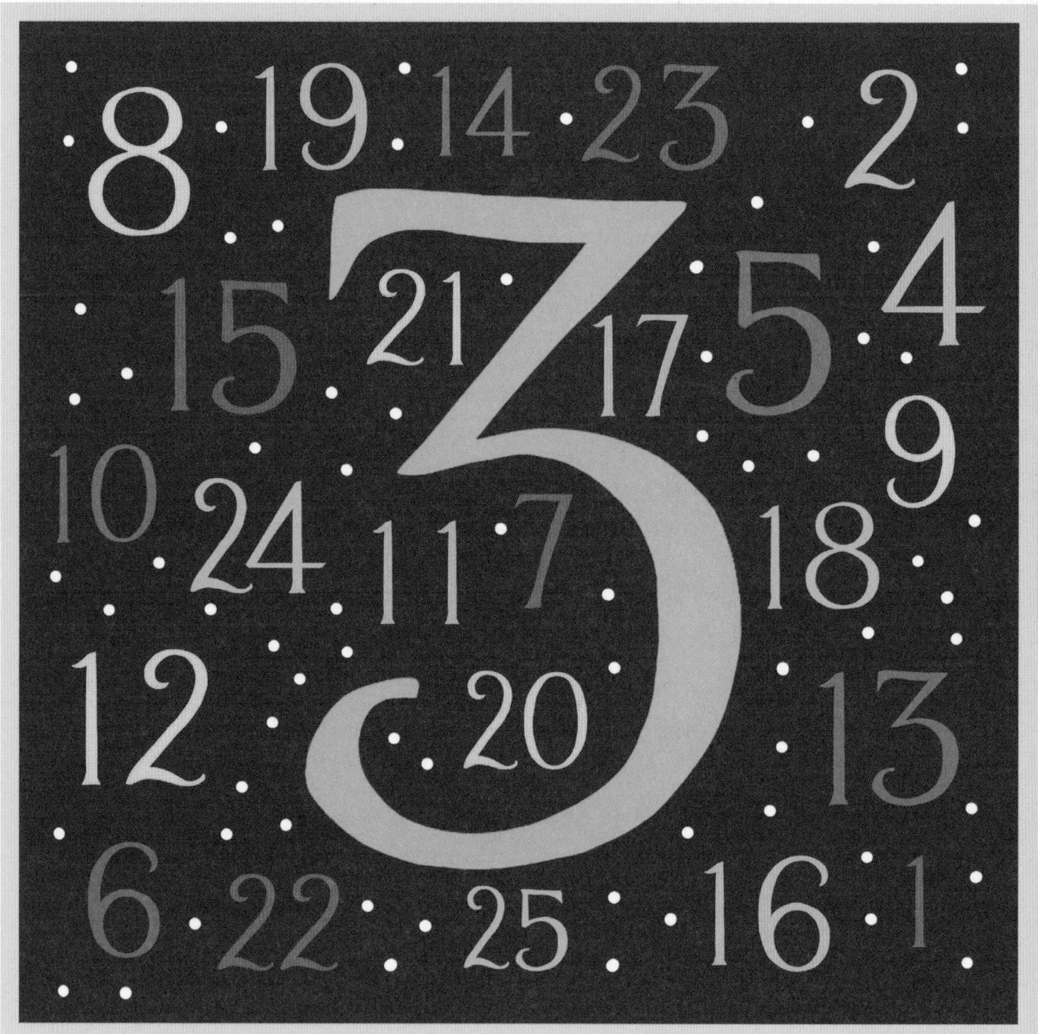
8
19
14
23
2
3
15
21
17
5
4
9
10
24
11
7
18
12
20
13
6
22
25
16
1

Alternative Advent Calendars

I love Advent calendars, but these days I want something a little more eco-friendly than the shop-bought chocolate-filled ones which are usually only partly recyclable and so add to your Christmas waste. Instead try out some of these greener versions. You can still have chocolate if you want – after all, there isn't anything wrong with breakfast chocolate when it's Christmas!

Reusable Advent Calendars

If you invest in a wooden or fabric Advent calendar, you'll be able to bring it out year after year. It can even be passed on as an heirloom to the next generation, if you look after it.

Have a look in your local charity shop and on local selling sites/pages, or ask friends and family if they have one they no longer want. We have a wooden calendar that I love, with a drawer for each day.

You could have a go at making one yourself too. It can be as simple as brown envelopes with a handwritten number on, pegged to a length of twine. Or hessian bags hung on the tree.

If you don't want a physical Advent calendar, you could write down all the things you want to do this Christmas on separate pieces of paper, mix them in up in a jar or box and pick a new one out each day. Another option would be to just have all your ideas in a list. Get creative and do what will work for you and your family. Remember, it's meant to be fun!

Filling an Advent calendar

What I love about a homemade and reusable Advent calendar is that there are so many ways to fill it. It can provide a moment of calm or excitement depending on what you choose for each day. It's good to mix it up!

In our wooden calendar drawers, I place a little piece of paper with a Christmassy activity written on it for us to do that day. We spend the month of December doing all sorts of Christmas-themed crafts, going on outings and playing games.

If this is something you're interested in, but you're worried it's just going to end up being yet another item on your to-do list, maybe only pick a couple of activities to start out with and put little objects behind all the other doors. Tailor your Advent calendar to you.

Some ideas to fill the kids' Advent calendars could be chocolate coins, Lego figures (these are easy to source second hand), nice writing paper for writing Santa a letter, play dough (see Homemade No-cook Play Dough on page 93), seeds, a new pencil or wooden toys.

Adults might enjoy finding chocolate, jokes, riddles, an I-owe-you voucher or maybe even a homemade mulled wine spice kit or a small succulent (see page 58 for how to propagate your own) as a bigger treat at the end.

If you're doing activities, make them as simple or as elaborate as you like. Write the activities for that day onto a scrap of paper, or you could even make tiny scrolls tied with ribbon. Add suspense by drawing a clue for a Christmas-themed surprise that will be happening later that day. Here are some ideas to get you started:

- An invitation: to visit Santa

- A sheet of writing paper: writing Santa a letter

- A bauble: decorating the tree – make an evening of it

- A paper snowflake: doing a craft activity like making snowflakes or popcorn strings to help decorate the house (turn to the Decorations chapter on page 105 for other craft ideas)

- A Scrabble letter: games night that evening with all your favourite board games

- A bottle of wine: date night with a picnic or tapas by the tree

- A musical note: making a Christmas playlist together full of your Christmas favourites to be played throughout December

- Popcorn: a movie night in with your favourite Christmas film and snacks

- A biscuit: baking Gingerbread Christmas Biscuits together (see page 43)

- A bird: making a winter feeder to feed the birds and squirrels

- A nature trail or a map: for a winter walk

Different Advent Calendars

If you are looking for a totally different style of Advent calendar, one that is less focused on receiving but that still counts down to Christmas, then there are many more ideas.

Decluttering calendar

This is exactly what it says: a way to declutter in the run-up to Christmas. The easiest version is to find at least one item each day that you no longer want or need. At the end of the 24 days you will have 24 items to sell, give to friends, swap or donate.

Reverse Advent calendar

A reverse Advent calendar consists of collecting long-life food items and toiletries which you then donate at the end of the 24 days. You could add one item per day or donate as many as you like and are able to. You could also create a reverse Advent with a group of friends or family and add one item per person per day.

Pay-it-forward calendar

With a pay-it-forward calendar the idea is to do something kind each day. Maybe you pay for the next person's coffee in the coffee queue or you donate some warm clothing to a homeless shelter. The possibilities are endless!

Book Advent

Simply gather up all the Christmas books and stories that you have. You don't need to wrap the books up, just pop them in a basket by the fireplace or under the tree. Have a look for some short stories and poems, and try to read something different each night – or pick out some special picture books if you have kids. You could collect extra books from the library or buy them second-hand to add to your festive library each year.

Advent candle

Christmas calendar candles are printed with the numbers 1 to 24. Each day in December the candle is burned down a little more, to show the passing of the days leading up to Christmas. Traditionally in Denmark and Germany, where they originate, the Advent candle is lit during a family meal each day. As the candle gets shorter, Christmas gets nearer. On Christmas Eve you let it burn out completely.

Charity calendars

If you want to buy an Advent calendar, charity calendars are such a great option. Usually, the money that you have bought the calendar with is donated to 24 different charities. Each door reveals a different donation, from feeding the homeless to protecting our oceans and endangered animals. You can do something amazing each day!

Christmas Cards

Christmas cards have lost their popularity over recent years. There is no doubt that they cause a lot of waste, with estimates of over 1.5 billion being thrown away each year, but I'm not here to tell you to stop sending them altogether! There are plenty of eco-friendly options for you to choose from, as well as alternative ideas such as friendship cards, which get passed back and forth. When Christmas is over, you can either recycle or compost the cards you've received, or turn them into decorations and gift tags for next year.

Sustainable Christmas Cards

My family and I used to send a Christmas card to every single person we knew, which produced a lot of waste and meant we spent a lot of money on stamps and cards. Now I tend to send e-cards or create homemade cards.

If you are looking to buy traditional cards, however, there are some sustainable options. These are the things to look out for:

- ★ Choose cards that are Forest Stewardship Council (FSC) certified. This ensures the paper used has been sustainably and ethically produced.

- ★ Avoid glittery cards because they can't be recycled.

- ★ Try to buy plastic-free cards wrapped in paper rather than cellophane, or even naked cards without wrapping.

- ★ Buy cards printed with vegetable inks. Look for the 'printed with vegetable-based inks' stamp.

- ★ Buy a card that gives back. Some companies will plant a tree for every card sold, or will give money from your purchase to a charity.

- ★ Go digital. Plenty of online sites now give you the chance to make and personalise your own cards, without the carbon footprint.

- ★ Plantable paper cards embedded with flower, herb or even vegetable seeds make a lovely gift. Your recipient can sow the seeds in the spring.

Friendship cards and newsletters

A friendship card gets passed back and forth. One person starts it and writes a little note, and the next year the recipient sends it back to you with an added little note. You can keep the card going for as long as you like. It means you will have to be careful not to lose it, but what a lovely keepsake you will end up with, in years to come.

My parents also use Christmas as an opportunity to catch up with old friends, sending a letter updating them on everything that has happened that year. With social media, we do tend to keep up with each other's lives more easily. But if you're trying to step away from social media, this is a lovely way to revert to the written word.

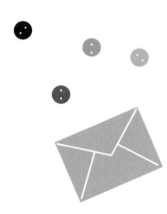

Button-and-Ribbon Christmas Cards

Creating a fabulous-looking card from some ribbon and buttons won't cost much at all. Source your materials from charity shops or use any you have lying around at home. Velvet ribbon gives the most luxurious-looking finish. Opt for Kraft card as it is already made from recycled materials and adds a lovely rustic vibe.

YOU WILL NEED

Card and envelope

Glue – eco-friendly, water-based, in recycled or recyclable packaging

Ribbon (any material and colour)

Buttons (any shapes and colours you want)

HOW TO MAKE

1 Mark out a line in the middle of the card, the length that you want your tree to be, and glue down one end of the ribbon where the base of the tree will be.

2 Once the ribbon is secure, create a loop, add more glue a bit higher up the line, about 1cm, and secure the loop. Keep going back and forth up the length of the line, with the loops getting smaller the higher up you go to create a Christmas tree shape.

4 Once the glue is fully dry, decorate the trunk of your tree with buttons. This will help to further secure the ribbon and create a tree trunk. You could also use one to create a star for the top of the tree.

5 Write a Christmas greeting underneath your tree with calligraphy or hand lettering. Check out Pinterest for ideas and experiment first!

The Giving
of Gifts

Giving gifts is a lovely thing. It shows people that we care about them. I often prefer giving to receiving – seeing someone open a gift you have made, or thought carefully about, can be more exciting than opening one yourself.

If you really think about what you're gifting, it becomes a much more enjoyable and sustainable experience. Rather than buying a present just for the sake of it, and likely one that's unwanted, instead give something the recipient will treasure and use. You will certainly prevent some of the huge amount of waste created by unwanted Christmas gifts each year.

Secret Santa

Secret Santa is a great option if you want to reduce your gift giving among a group of people: it's simply a case of picking out names from a hat (or using an app) and buying a present for the person you picked, instead of everyone giving presents to everyone. The idea is that the gifter is anonymous, so all the presents are from 'Santa'. There are so many ways you can do this, but the one rule I would recommend sticking to is a spending limit! It really doesn't have to be high. You might also like to try a themed Secret Santa where the gifts all have to be sustainable.

Get together to swap your gifts in the traditional way or you could even do a treasure hunt to find them.

Conscious Gifting

Conscious gifting is when you really think about whether the person will enjoy and/or benefit from the gift you are giving. You aren't just giving for the sake of it. Sometimes it's tempting to give a person something you want them to like, rather than finding a gift that they will truly enjoy and make use of!

If you are really unsure of what to get someone, you could always ask them. Perhaps you could come up with some ideas of things to do together.

How to choose a gift

There is always someone who already has everything! This is especially true today, when we're used to receiving whatever we want the next day, thanks to a few clicks of the mouse. So how do you come up with a unique gift?

- ★ Think about any hobbies they have. Is there something you could get them that's related to their hobby – maybe an experience linked to it or some new kit?

- ★ For books, ask them what their favourite genre is in conversation and go from there.

- ★ Are they studying or at school? Something like new stationery or a nice notebook will be a lovely, useful gift.

- ★ If you know their favourite music, you could get them some second-hand vinyl, or perhaps a book about that style of music or a favourite artist.

- ★ How do they feel about the environment? Would they wish to receive only items that are zero-waste or cruelty-free?

- ★ For toys, opt for long-lasting timeless versions that can be passed on once they have been outgrown.

- ★ Make sure any clothing is the correct size and style for them. If in doubt, don't get it!

Create memories

Often experiences provide more joy than objects. An experience is the ultimate zero-waste gift! You could even gift experiences to do together, so you'll be sure to spend some quality time with each other. For example:

- Tickets to a show
- Netflix subscription
- Membership to the National Trust
- Donation to a charity they really care about
- Tickets to a gig
- Camping trip
- Cookery course
- Calligraphy class
- Spa day
- Adrenalin experience, such as bungee jumping or skydiving

- Cinema vouchers
- Restaurant vouchers or a restaurant experience
- Challenge experience, such as an escape room
- Water sports: maybe they want to try paddle-boarding, canoeing or wakeboarding
- Distillery visit
- Afternoon tea
- Crafting workshop
- Photography tour or class

- Promises: a promise of a coffee date paid for by you; a promise of a surprise picnic one day in the summer; a promise of a hiking trip they have always wanted to go on; a promise of a night of babysitting, etc.

The Art of Asking for Sustainable Gifts

If you regularly talk about your journey to a greener lifestyle, people close to you will no doubt know to give you a gift that's in alignment with your beliefs and passions. I know not to buy my vegetarian sister a food gift that she couldn't eat, for example.

My relatives will often ask me for ideas when it comes to buying gifts for my children. I always request no large plastic toys and maybe suggest something they need. We've asked for camping equipment in the past, or experiences like a membership to somewhere.

Gift givers will much prefer to know what you would like than to end up giving you a present you don't like. So don't be afraid to tell them beforehand – you could even make a list of ideas, and request the same from the people close to you. Of course, if you do still end up receiving a gift you don't want to or can't use, accept it graciously, put it to one side and decide what to do with it later. You can always donate or re-gift it (see the Re-gifting section on page 69).

How to Talk about Non-gifting

If you want to cut down on the number of gifts, find out how your friends and family would feel about this. Some people love gift giving. It's probably going to be a bit of an awkward conversation, but you might be surprised that both sides end up relieved.

How you approach the conversation is going to depend on your relationship with the person in question and how you think they will respond to it. There is no one-size-fits-all answer for this.

If you can broach the subject early enough that they won't have already bought presents (late November is too late) then go for it! Give some time to thinking about how you want to start the conversation. Some ideas you might find useful are given opposite.

★ Explain your reasoning behind wanting to gift fewer physical items. If it is due to financial reasons, be honest and say that you are cutting right back. Another approach is to share articles about the problems of unwanted gifts. There are so many of these on social media, or forward an email or meme. This is an easy way to open up the issue for discussion.

★ Bring up and talk about a happy memory you have shared. Suggest that you could enjoy a similar experience together in lieu of a physical gift. It will also give you both something to look forward to.

★ If you often get the same style of present from someone that you really don't want, it's okay to let them know your tastes have changed or that you have stopped a particular hobby – and remember that kids have changing tastes too.

Creative
Gifts

Creative gifts can require a little more thought than simply grabbing something off a shelf, but the anticipation of giving something homemade can be so exciting! And not only can they be more environmentally friendly but they usually end up cheaper too. Here I've rounded up four of my favourite creative gift ideas for you to try. Try to choose organic and fairtrade ingredients for all recipes in the book where possible.

Gingerbread Christmas Biscuits

These gingerbread biscuits are a classic bake at Christmas time. You could gift these on their own or as part of a hamper. They can also be used as edible gift tags, decorations for the tree or even name places for your Christmas dinner table. Have a look for Christmas-themed cookie cutters in local second-hand shops or on selling pages. Or if you are buying new, make sure you get good-quality metal cutters for longevity.

YOU WILL NEED

320g plain flour, plus extra for rolling

1 teaspoon bicarbonate of soda

2 teaspoons ground ginger

100g light soft brown sugar

100g unsalted butter, softened

4 tablespoons golden syrup

1 large free-range egg, beaten

Christmas cookie cutters

Icing and decorations (optional)

Twine or ribbon, if making into gift tags or decorations

HOW TO MAKE

1   Sift the flour, bicarbonate of soda and ginger into a bowl. Add the brown sugar and mix together well.

2   Put the butter and golden syrup into a small saucepan over a low heat until it's just melted. Don't allow it to boil.

3   Pour the melted mixture into your bowl with the flour and sugar and mix everything together. Next add the beaten egg and mix again. Once it is all mixed, use your hands to knead it into a smooth dough.

4   Take the dough out of the bowl and wrap in a tea towel or a beeswax wrap and chill in the fridge for 15 minutes.

5   Preheat the oven to 200°C/ 180°C fan/gas mark 6. Line two baking trays with non-stick baking paper and lightly dust a work surface with flour.

6   Remove your dough from the fridge and cut it in half. Return one half to the fridge and roll the rest out to the thickness of a £1 coin. Use your cookie cutters to cut the dough into shapes and then place them on the prepared baking trays. If you are planning to use these as tree decorations or gift tags, make a small hole in each biscuit before baking them.

7 Bake your gingerbread biscuits for 10–12 minutes, or until they have turned golden brown. Keep checking on them so that they don't burn.

8 Remove them from the oven and allow to cool for a few minutes before transferring to a wire rack to cool completely.

9 Repeat with the remaining dough.

10 Once your Gingerbread Christmas Biscuits have cooled you can decorate them how you want. They look nice with icing around the edges and little silver balls.

11 If you are using these as decorations or gifts tags, once the icing has dried, carefully thread through some ribbon or twine. Or put a few into a Mason jar and tie with twine for a delicious gift. They should keep for 2–3 weeks if stored in an airtight container, so they can be made in advance.

Easy Chocolate Fudge

Chocolate fudge is so easy to make and is really yummy. You can make it either in a slow cooker or microwave, or by creating a bain marie. With so many different variations, it makes a fab gift for Christmas – simply place some in a paper bag, Mason jar or tin. You could even include it in a Christmas hamper with other homemade gifts.

YOU WILL NEED

400g chocolate (see variations opposite)

1 tin of condensed milk (for a vegan option, use coconut or soya condensed milk)

2 tablespoons butter (or vegan butter)

HOW TO MAKE

1   Break the chocolate into pieces, then put all the ingredients into the slow cooker or a heatproof bowl if using a microwave or bain marie. The trick is to not overheat it and to stir the chocolate in as it melts.

2   Slow cooker times may vary but I put it on high for an hour, stirring every 10 minutes. If you are using a microwave, put it on high for 10-second bursts, stirring in between. For a bain marie, place the bowl over a pan of simmering water, making sure the bottom of the bowl doesn't touch the water. Stir until the chocolate has melted.

3   Line a baking tray with non-stick baking paper and pour the fudge mixture in. Leave it to cool and then place in the fridge to set overnight, or for at least 4 hours. Once set you can cut it into squares.

Variations of fudge to try

CHOCOLATE ORANGE

300g milk chocolate and 100g dark orange chocolate, with 50g grated orange chocolate on top. Grate the chocolate on top once the fudge is in the baking tray.

WHITE CHOC CHIPS

300g milk chocolate and 100g white chocolate, topped with a handful of white chocolate chips (scatter these on once the fudge mixture has been poured into the tray).

CARAMEL

100g milk chocolate and 300g white chocolate, with a tin of caramel condensed milk instead of regular condensed milk.

OREOS

300g white chocolate and 100g cookies-and-cream chocolate, with 4–6 crushed Oreos. Stir the crushed Oreos into the fudge mixture before pouring into the tray.

MINT AERO

100g milk chocolate and 200g dark chocolate, with 100g mint Aero. Break the Aero into little pieces and swirl through the fudge before placing in the fridge to set.

Tin-Can Planters

These upcycled tin-can planters make a really unique gift. They can be made with any used tins, for example, chopped tomato tins. With a little creativity, you can make them match any décor. They look great as a set lined up in a row on a shelf and they can also be used as outdoor planters.

YOU WILL NEED

1 tin (or as many as you want to make)

Eco paint – water- and rust-resistant (I usually pick a pale neutral colour to complement the twine, but you can choose any colour based on your colour scheme)

Twine or ribbon

Glue – eco-friendly, water-based, in recycled or recyclable packaging

Small rocks or stones, enough to fill a third of the tin

Soil, enough to fill half the tin – either from your garden or multi-purpose peat-free compost

Succulents or other small plants

HOW TO MAKE

1   Start by prepping the tin. Make sure it's free of any metal shards left over from opening it. Then wash it well, removing any labels, and dry it. If you are struggling to remove sticky glue residue, you can apply white vinegar, leave it for a couple of minutes and then scrape it off with a knife.

2   Next, paint the inside of your tin. You can simply focus on the top section. Let it dry thoroughly before flipping to paint the outside with an even layer. Let it dry again. It's best to do this outside if you can, to avoid getting paint inside the house. Or lay down an old towel or newspaper before you start.

3   To decorate the planter, wrap the twine around the top of the can a few times and fix it in place with some glue. Alternatively, you could wrap around some ribbon.

4   Fill the bottom third of the tin with small rocks or stones, for drainage. Add the soil, making a hole in which to place your plant. Carefully place your plant in the hole and then gently pack the soil around it. Dust off any excess soil.

5   Tie on a brown paper tag to give as a little gift.

Brown-Sugar Scrub

Making DIY beauty products can be so much fun, and they are better for you too. I much prefer using natural ingredients on my skin. All the ingredients here can easily be found in the shops (and you might already have them in your kitchen cupboards).

This brown-sugar scrub is quick and easy to make. It's a great – inexpensive – gift you can give to teachers, friends or new mums, use as a stocking filler, or gift it to yourself!

The mixture of the brown sugar, a natural exfoliator, and the moisturising oil makes skin silky smooth. It is gentle enough to use on your face too.

A note on the oil: choose a neutral-smelling oil. I personally like coconut oil because it makes the scrub creamier and it has a delicious smell. You could also use almond oil or grapeseed oil. I'd avoid olive oil unless you don't mind its strong smell. Also avoid any nut oils if you have allergies.

YOU WILL NEED

2 cups brown sugar (if you want a grainer texture, use demerara, or for a smoother texture, use soft brown sugar)

1 cup solid (but soft) coconut oil

A few drops of essential oils of your choice (vanilla, cinnamon or nutmeg are all lovely)

1 sealable glass jar (I like to use Mason jars because they're easy to clean and reuse)

Twine or ribbon, to decorate

Gift tag

HOW TO MAKE

1   Place all the ingredients in a food processor and blend together for a couple of minutes. If you don't have a food processor, you can also mix them together in a bowl with a wooden spoon. It will be easier if your sugar is fresh so there are no lumps.

2   If the mixture starts to separate, don't panic. Leave it for a while and mix again. (This will also happen if the scrub is left in a warm place like the shower. Just use a clean finger to mix it together before using.)

3   Once your sugar scrub is mixed, spoon it into a clean jar.

4   Decorate your jar of scrub with some twine or ribbon. Add a little gift tag with the name of the scrub and the ingredients.

Homegrown Gifts

If you have plants at home or grow your own vegetables, fruit, herbs or flowers, then you have some lovely natural and sustainable gift options. There are so many possibilities and you can really tailor your homegrown gifts to the lucky recipient's tastes. Package up some herbs or spices, put together a whole hamper of homegrown items or even create a themed package.

Edible Christmas Gifts from the Garden

Chillies

Gift a spice lover some homegrown chillies. They can either be dried or fresh – or even give them a chilli plant that you have cultivated yourself. Another idea would be to give some chilli seeds and little pots for growing them in, along with a chilli cookbook.

Dried herbs

Herbs from your herb garden make a lovely gift. Rosemary and bay leaves work particularly well. Simply place into glass jars and add a gift tag. You could even include a hand-written favourite recipe that uses the herbs.

TO DRY YOUR HERBS:

1 Cut healthy stems from your herbs.

2 Remove any dead leaves and clear the bottom of each stem.

3 Shake gently to remove any bugs or debris.

4 Bundle 4–5 stems together and tie with twine.

5 Hang them upside down in a warm, airy room for at least two weeks.

6 Once your herbs are dry, place them into airtight glass jars.

Preserving

Jams, pickles and chutneys are always a welcome gift. Try some preserving this year and you can create a whole range of homegrown gifts that will last.

- Chutneys are great for accompanying the Christmas after-dinner cheeseboard, but you can also add them to other dishes like roasts or even to scrambled eggs at breakfast.

- Pickles are a perfect gift for those without a sweet tooth. Pickle some of your homegrown onions, cucumbers or courgettes. There are so many pickling options!

- Making jam from a glut of strawberries is an easy way to save them from going to waste and is a tasty treat with fresh bread for breakfast. Include a pot in a breakfast-themed hamper.

Cordials

Cordials can be added to fizzy water for a refreshing drink, or create a delicious Christmas cocktail by adding to a dash of gin topped up with Prosecco. Rhubarb works well or try to forage some elderflowers.

Themed packages

If you want to put together some themed packages, there are so many lovely ideas. You can really get inventive and tailor them to people's likes.

- Gift seeds along with a book on how to grow them and maybe even some little gardening tools.

- Make infused oils in glass bottles and gift along with a second-hand herb chopping board, herb cutter and book about herbs from the charity shop.

- Create a spice mix in a jar and gift along with a hand-written favourite family recipe.

- Place some dried flowers from your garden in a glass jar along with other ingredients for a natural beauty product, and include instructions for how to make it.

- Create a breakfast-themed hamper with freshly baked bread, jam, fairtrade coffee and maybe even a bottle of fizz.

Propagating Plantlets

If you have a plant at home, you can almost always make lots of plant babies from it. Give these plantlets to your friends and family for a thoughtful living gift that costs very little.

Don't panic, you don't have to be an expert in propagating plants! I have included some simple methods here. Don't worry about damaging your plants; clipping will encourage them to grow new stems.

The best time to propagate your large-leafed plants is during the spring and summer months when they are actively growing. You can propagate your succulents at any time, as long as you have a sunny windowsill, although growth may be slower during the winter months. Follow these easy steps, allow enough time and you will have some plantlets ready to be transferred to their new homes in time for Christmas. So find some pots from your local charity shop or selling pages – you could even use your upcycled tin-can planters (see page 48) – and get propagating.

For **succulents** like Sedum or Graptopetalum varieties, use leaf cuttings.

1 To take a leaf for propagation, gently twist the leaf off the stem. Make sure it's a clean pull, leaving nothing on the stem. It's okay to pull off a little of the stem too.

2 Next fill a plate or baking tray with soil and place your leaf cuttings on top. Make sure their cut ends don't actually touch the soil at all. Place on a sunny windowsill and wait for around 3 days for them to scab over where they have been detached from the stem. Once they have scabbed over, water the leaves each time the soils dries out with a spray bottle.

3 After a few weeks, new roots and a rosette (the new succulent plant) will start to grow. After 3–4 weeks, the new plants will be large enough to pot into their new homes. Nestle the new roots into soil with the rosette sitting on top. You can place the old leaf into the soil along with the roots or remove it.

For **large-leafed plants** like monsteras, otherwise known as the Swiss cheese plant, and philodendrons, including the sweetheart plant, use stem cuttings.

These plants have a tendency to grow and grow, so propagating is a good way to encourage them to grow in the way you want, rather than them taking over your room.

1   Find the node: choose a section of stem that has one or more leaves and that includes at least one node, which will look like a little brown plant spot. A section of stem around 20cm long with 2–3 nodes offers plenty of opportunities to sprout new roots and leaves, but you can propagate a new plant from 5cm of stem as long as it has a node.

2   With sharp scissors, carefully snip your chosen stem. Make sure to cut your stem diagonally below a root or leaf node.

3   Place your sections of stem into clear jars of water so that you can easily see the root growth without having to disturb the plant.

4   Keep the plants in indirect sunlight, and only change the water if it starts looking too cloudy or it needs topping up.

5   Growing roots can take anywhere from a couple weeks to a few months. When your plant babies are strong, with substantial root systems, pot them with fresh soil into their new homes.

6   Make sure they have enough room to continue growing but not too much or they might fall over.

Pre-loved Gifts

I have been buying second-hand – or pre-loved as I prefer to call it – Christmas gifts for years now. There are so many items being sold that have hardly been used. Sometimes you can even find completely new items with a tag still on.

I get a real thrill from finding the perfect pre-loved gift, usually at a fraction of its normal retail price. It is also nice to know that if I find something in a charity shop, the money I spend will do some good.

How To Buy Pre-loved Gifts

By shopping second-hand, you're helping to create a more circular economy, reducing demand for new Christmas one-off items and lowering your overall environmental impact.

I know some people wouldn't be keen to give or receive a pre-loved gift and I think that's due to a bit of stigma around used things. Luckily, more and more people are seeing second-hand shopping as being normal. When you think about it, doesn't it seem ridiculous to fork out for a brand-new item when you can get a six-month-old barely used pre-loved version for a tenth of the price?

When it comes to buying pre-loved gifts, there are ways to ensure you get the best items in the best condition and at the best prices:

Look in more than one place. Look in person in charity shops or go online. Check the main reselling sites like eBay but also look on sites like Gumtree and Freecycle, and your local selling pages and Marketplace on Facebook.

Research an item before buying it. What does it normally sell for? Are you making much of a saving? Does it have all the parts you need? These are just some of the questions you should know the answers to before making that purchase.

Consider upcycling. Upcycling is 'doing up' an object or piece of furniture. This is a great option if you are crafty or looking to create something really personal.

If you're buying online, search for items using the 'nearest first' tool. This enables you to see results in order of how close they are to you. The more local the item is, the lower your carbon footprint and if you can collect it, you will save on more packaging and posting.

Go for gifts you know they will love. Sometimes the price of a new item puts you off, even if you know someone would love it. Instead search for a second-hand version and see if it is now possible. Of course, make sure you aren't just buying something because it is a bargain.

Don't be afraid to offer a lower price for items out of your price range. The worst that can happen is that they say no!

Check the sizing carefully if you are buying second-hand clothing. Then make sure that they are freshly washed or dry-cleaned before gifting them.

When buying books, check bestseller lists and look for books that have recently come out. Opt for books that are in a good condition; often you can't tell they have already been read.

Give yourself time. If you are looking around charity shops, it often requires a good rummage to find the best items. Also allow time for postage of items if you are buying them from online selling sites, as they are unlikely to arrive the next day!

Think about themed items. Maybe you see some vintage wine glasses that you could pair with a nice bottle of organic wine. Or a book you could put into a care package with a bath-bomb and some organic chocolate.

My favourite items to buy pre-loved

Whenever I am searching for a gift, I always look for second-hand items first. I have successfully bought all of these pre-loved:

- Clothing or accessories like shoes and handbags, particularly designer labels that you can get at a fraction of their original retail price
- Books
- Vinyl
- Toys (wooden toys, board games, Lego and educational games are always popular)
- Crockery and glassware
- Electronics (mobile phones, handheld gaming devices, etc.)
- Gardening items
- Outdoor toys
- Camping or outdoors equipment
- Baby items

Re-gifting

The most eco-friendly way of living is to use something you already have, rather than buy new. This can be applied to your gift giving with re-gifting, which is when you give someone else a gift that has been given to you, but that you will never use or isn't to your taste. It is a great option, but it has to be done tactfully and carefully. Obviously the first rule of re-gifting is to not give it back to the person who gave it to you!

Don't re-gift anything meaningful or handmade. People will be upset if they have spent time creating or thinking about a gift for you, only to find out you have given it away. Instead, try to appreciate the time and effort they have spent on you.

Re-gift outside your family or circle of friends. You don't want the person whose gift you have re-gifted to spot it in someone else's house.

Re-gift thoughtfully. Don't simply re-gift an item to get rid of it! Your gift still needs to be thoughtful (see Conscious Gifting on page 34 for some tips).

Carefully check. Make sure there is nothing left over from when you were given the present, such as a card or tag with your name on.

Make sure it won't be missed. If you think there is any chance the gift giver could ask how you are getting on with it or where something is that they have given you, then it comes under the 'meaningful gift' category and you probably shouldn't re-gift it. Or wait a while before doing so.

Wrapping Paper

When it comes to wrapping presents, it's very easy to get caught up in all the glitter and sparkles at this time of year. But sadly the sparkly wrapping paper that I used to favour isn't recyclable. Most Christmas wrapping paper isn't! Glitter, synthetic inks, plastic coating and sticky tape can mean gift wrap ends up in landfill instead.

It's estimated that every Christmas in the UK we throw away enough wrapping paper to circle the entire globe nine times. That is a huge amount of waste. But don't panic, there are lots of eco-friendly gift-wrapping ideas that are better for the environment – and probably your pocket too.

Customising Brown Paper

Grab yourself a roll of recycled brown paper and you can be eco-friendly and as creative as you like in your wrapping.

- Draw on your own bows.

- Stamp your brown paper with Christmas-themed stamps and ink. The kids can even get involved in this one.

- If you can do calligraphy, it's a simple but effective way to decorate your brown-paper-wrapped parcels. Just write the recipient's name in beautiful writing, perhaps with a Christmas message. This also does away with the need for tags.

- Use a white pen to draw on some pretty snowflakes.

- See the Ribbons and Tags chapter (page 77) for more ideas on how to embellish a package.

Save and Reuse

My mum used to laboriously pick off the sticky tape from gifts and save the wrapping paper to use again. When I was younger I used to think it was such a waste of time. But I think she was ahead of the curve. I now always keep a stash of old wrapping paper, various-sized gift bags and ribbons and bows from gifts throughout the year, which I store together in a box.

It's become a standing joke in my family that the gift bags get passed around with lots of, 'Ooh, what a lovely gift bag this is' on Christmas morning or birthdays!

Don't forget those free newspapers that are posted through your letter box. They make surprisingly beautiful wrapping paper (just check the headlines first).

If you head down to your local charity shop, you'll find lots more options. Old maps make wonderful wrapping paper, especially if you can find one with personal significance. Scarves and tea towels work as fabric wrapping (see Wrap with Fabric opposite) and jars, biscuit tins and cotton bags are all handy too.

And if you really want to buy some Christmas paper, you could have a look for some that's locally made, ideally from recycled waste with pulp that hasn't been bleached. You can also opt for paper that is printed with vegetable inks and delivered in recycled brown envelopes. Yes, there really are some great companies out there!

Wrap with Fabric

One way to wrap a present with fabric is to use it much like you would regular wrapping paper and just secure it with a ribbon. Or have a go at furoshiki, a Japanese wrapping tradition using fabric cloths that are made to be reused. Furoshiki was first used to protect precious items but has grown in popularity recently as an eco-friendly way of wrapping.

Source retro tea towels and pretty scarves from charity shops, online vintage sellers or haberdasheries. Or buy purpose-made furoshiki material kits.

You could also include a note with the gift, giving instructions on how to reuse the fabric.

BOOK CARRY WRAP Great for books and boxed gifts.

BOTTLE CARRY WRAP Makes a perfectly wrapped gift for a party and is a great way to carry bottles to a picnic. You can do this with one or two bottles.

Ribbons and Tags

Now you have your eco-wrapping sorted (thanks to the Wrapping Paper chapter on pages 71–5), don't spoil it by using sticky tape! Sticky tape cannot be recycled in the UK, meaning Christmas Day can create an enormous amount of waste headed directly for landfill. And don't forget your ribbons, string and tags too, which often get lost in the pile of paper and thrown away.

Tying Gifts

Instead of buying new ribbons every Christmas, save them throughout the year and add them to your wrapping box. Charity shops are also a great place to look for second-hand ribbons. I love finding big, thick velvet and satin ribbons to add to my collection. When it comes to Christmas wrapping, you will have a variety of lengths and colours to choose from.

You could always ask the recipients of your beautifully tied gifts to keep hold of the ribbons to either give back to you or reuse themselves.

Another option is to tie your present together with twine, either the rustic kind or a pretty colourful one. If you use brown paper, wrap it in the traditional way and make sure to fold your creases firmly to help secure its shape.

STICKY OPTIONS

We now know that plastic sticky tape can contribute to a huge amount of waste going to landfill. However, if you do feel you need a sticky option, choose tape that is recycled, biodegradable and made out of natural materials. Paper tape or paper stickers can be composted or recycled. You could even personalise them to create a truly individual look! And you won't need to laboriously remove them from any recyclable wrapping paper.

Washi tape is another option, as it is typically made from hemp and bamboo and the self-adhesive is compostable and recyclable too. Just factor in air miles here and try to order washi tape that has been made in the UK.

Embellishing a Gift

Decorate your gifts with unique details instead of relying on sticky decorations that get chucked away straight after Christmas.

* Head down to your local charity shop and have a dig through the jewellery and ornaments for decorative things to attach to your presents. They can be reused next year, or turned into decorations for the tree.

* Get outside and forage for clippings to tie on with string or ribbon. Some favourites are holly leaves, pine cones, rosemary and winterberries. Or use some small cuttings from your Christmas tree, if it's a real one. You could even add a sprig of mistletoe for that special someone!

* For gorgeous-smelling and pretty-looking presents, dry some orange slices and pair these with a few cinnamon sticks. Have a look at how to dry orange slices later in this chapter (see Dried-Orange Gift Tags on page 83).

Gift Tags

One year I tried wrapping without gift tags and it didn't turn out as well as I had planned. I thought I would remember whose was whose from the shape alone, but I couldn't! It's much easier and less stressful to label your presents, whether with a tag or written onto the wrapping paper itself. If you want to use a gift tag, there are plenty of green options.

* Use brown-card luggage labels. These can easily be recycled or composted, and you can write on them with pretty lettering, or use inks and Christmas stamps.

* Keep your old Christmas cards, or find vintage ones in charity shops and create tags out of them.

* For the ultimate tag you can make salt-dough gift tags that can be used year after year. Just remember to take them off and store them somewhere safe! See page 84 for how to make them.

* You could try a gingerbread gift tag as an edible alternative. See the Gingerbread Christmas Biscuits recipe on page 43.

Dried-Orange Gift Tags

These dried orange slices are really versatile. You can hang them on your tree, add them to presents with twine for a natural look or make an orange garland.

YOU WILL NEED

Oranges

A knife

A wire rack, or baking sheet lined with baking paper

Twine or ribbon

HOW TO MAKE

1 Slice your oranges horizontally to about 1cm wide. Make an incision near the outer edge of each slice. This is for your ribbon or twine once your slices have dried.

2 Preheat the oven to the lowest possible setting. Arrange the orange slices on a wire rack or lined baking sheet. They will dry more quickly and be less sticky on a wire rack, but a baking sheet will also work. Place in the oven for 4 hours, turning them every hour or so.

3 Remove from the oven and leave to cool. Don't worry if they feel a bit tacky at first, they will dry out.

4 Once they have cooled, to turn your dried orange slices into gift tags or decorations, feed either your ribbon or twine through the hole in the slice and tie the end.

5 If you are making a garland, thread the orange slices onto a length of twine. It's helpful to wrap the twine ends with a piece of tape to prevent it from unravelling.

Salt-Dough Gift Tags

Making salt-dough gift tags is a lovely way to personalise your presents. You can keep tags and reuse them year after year or turn them into tree decorations, making them a great sustainable option.

This is a fun activity to do with kids and it could even be one of your Advent calendar activities (see Filling an Advent Calendar on page 20). If you want to create salt-dough tree ornaments, the method is the same.

YOU WILL NEED

2 cups plain flour (organic, if possible)

1 cup table salt

3–4 cups water, more if needed

Food colouring, essential oils or eco-glitter (optional)

Cookie cutters (optional)

Reusable straw (optional)

Twine or ribbon

HOW TO MAKE

1 Combine the flour and salt and then add the water. Mix together well to create a dough. If it's too dry, add a little more water. Add your food colouring, essential oils or eco-glitter at this point, if using. (The tags do look lovely plain too.)

2 Knead the dough. If you have a mixer, use the dough hook to do the work for you. Otherwise, use your hands. For a really finished product, make sure you knead the dough until it is smooth. This should take about 10 minutes. (If you want to prepare your dough in advance it should last a few days in an airtight container.)

3 Roll out the dough to about 5mm thick. If you're using cookie cutters, cut out your chosen shapes. Otherwise simply cut into rectangles with a knife. If you want to add a personalisation like a fingerprint, handprint or stamped initials, now is the time to do it.

4 Using a reusable straw or a knife cut out a small circle where you want the top of the tag to be. Then place them on a lined baking sheet.

5 You can either let your salt dough air-dry for at least 48 hours or, if you are low on time, you can bake them in the oven on the lowest setting for a few hours. (You could even do these at the same time as your orange slices to save on energy – see page 83.)

6 Once they are fully dry, loop your twine or ribbon through the hole to create your gift tag. If you have added a fingerprint or a handprint, it's a nice idea to write the date or a note with a fine-point permanent marker on the back.

Green Christmas
with Kids

If you can relax into it and have time to enjoy it all, Christmas really is a wonderful time of year when you have children. But how do you avoid getting sucked into all that relentless consumerism? It's easier with adults to explain that you want to give less presents at Christmas but when your kids are used to piles of presents, how do you change that?

Getting the Kids Involved

My partner and I have gradually reduced the number of presents we give the kids at Christmas, but we've also really started thinking about *what* we get them rather than just buying for the sake of getting them MORE.

My advice would be to sit your kids down, if they are old enough, and explain what you are doing and why. Ask them to make a list for you of things they really want and need so that they feel involved. You can also encourage them to be involved in choosing useful gifts for other family members.

Just remember that it's very easy to feel pressured to keep up, even if you don't want to. I still sometimes find myself almost dragged into a last-minute panic-buying session, worrying that I haven't got them enough. Especially after talking to friends about all the presents they are buying for their children. You don't need to drastically change how you do Christmas for your kids all in one go. But if the mass consumerism at Christmas time has been making you feel uncomfortable, start with reducing the amount that you buy, buying more thoughtfully and making homemade gifts.

Gifts for Children

Every family tends to do their gift giving in different ways. But most have some smaller items from Santa in their stockings and larger presents under the tree. For under the tree, we follow this rule of thumb:

Something they want

Something to wear

Something they need

Something to read

Eco-friendly Stocking Fillers

It's tempting to fill Christmas stockings with masses of little plastic toys just for the sake it. So here are some eco-friendly ideas of what you could add instead:

- Christmas-smelling play dough (see page 93 for how to make Homemade No-Cook Play Dough)
- A little book or an activity book
- Wooden toys and games
- A satsuma
- Fairtrade chocolate
- Stationery – maybe they need a new pencil case for school, some new colouring pencils or a diary

- Cruelty-free, natural toiletries such as a bath bomb
- Reusable water bottle or lunch box
- Organic cotton or bamboo socks and pants
- A board game
- Pre-loved books and toys (see the Pre-loved Gifts chapter on page 63)
- A natural candle
- Gardening items

- Outdoors items (bouncy ball, skipping rope, butterfly kit)
- A new skill to learn – knitting, chess, coding
- A gift card
- Voucher for an experience – maybe a day out or for something like a skateboard lesson
- Adopt an animal or a wildlife group membership

Christmas Eve Box

A Christmas Eve box is a lovely tradition to have. Our box is really simple, but the kids love it. I have a reusable box that I get out every year. It flat-packs so we can easily store it, but you can make your own by wrapping a box with a lid in Christmas paper. I put ours under the tree for Christmas Eve and tend to include these items:

- New pyjamas, but not a specific Christmas pattern so that they can be worn throughout the winter

- New slippers or warm socks

- Handmade hot chocolate pot with marshmallows (I put some cocoa powder and marshmallows into little glass jars, one for each child)

- Reindeer food (we normally make this at our farm trip to see Santa and I keep it for the box; if you are making your own, just make sure it is safe for wildlife)

- Our Christmas Eve story that we share every year together and one new Christmas book that we add to the collection (the book is new to us but may be one I have found second-hand)

- A simple craft like paper snowflakes or Christmas colouring for a quieter activity, or baking (in which case I would put a few Christmas cookie cutters in so that the kids know we will be doing it)

- Treats: maybe some homemade fudge, a few cookies we have baked or popcorn kernels to pop together

- Sometimes I also add a Christmas bath bomb

Homemade No-Cook Play Dough

Kids will love this easy play dough that takes just minutes to make. It's my go-to recipe! You can store it in little glass Kilner jars and even make it into an activity by putting a mini rolling pin, some cutters and natural decorations into a box with the jar of play dough.

YOU WILL NEED

2 cups plain flour, plus extra for dusting

½ cup salt

2 tablespoons cream of tartar

2 tablespoons vegetable oil (baby oil and coconut oil work too)

Food colouring and scents (optional): for a Christmas-scented play dough I add a pinch of ground cinnamon and ginger (make sure you don't add too much so as not to put your kids off playing with it!)

1–1½ cups boiling water

HOW TO MAKE

1 Place the flour, salt, cream of tartar and oil in a large mixing bowl.

2 Add your colouring, if using, to the boiling water. Pour half the water into the bowl and stir everything together, then add a little more, stirring all the time, until all the water is used up.

3 Keep stirring until your play dough is combined; it may still be a bit sticky at this point. IMPORTANT: allow it to cool down before taking it out of the bowl, it will be hot!

4 Sprinkle your worktop with some extra flour, tip the dough out of the bowl and knead it vigorously for a couple of minutes until all the stickiness has gone.

5 Keep kneading until it is the perfect consistency. If it is still a bit sticky, then add a little more flour until it is just right. You want it soft, smooth and squishy.

6 Store your play dough in any airtight containers, or for a little gift try glass jars with screw-top lids.

The Tree

Oh, Christmas tree, oh, Christmas tree, how lovely are your branches! But which branches are best: real or fake? Christmas for me means a real tree, and sneakily sniffing its pine scent instantly making me feel Christmassy – it's pure, heady nostalgia. But personal preferences aside, there is often a big debate around what is best for the environment and it is worth doing your research. You could also consider the most eco-friendly option: a tree-free Christmas tree.

Artificial Trees

Climbing into the loft, dusting off your Christmas tree box and bringing it out along with memories of years gone by might be your favourite thing about Christmas. And if you do have an artificial tree, reusing it year after year is definitely the best thing to do.

The key problem with artificial trees is that they are made from plastic. The oil used in the manufacture of plastic trees and the industrial emissions produced are what creates its carbon footprint. They are also often shipped long distances before arriving in the shop and then your home.

Offsetting a fake tree's carbon footprint will take time. You would need to use your artificial tree for at least ten years for it to offset its carbon footprint. Some studies state it is actually more like 20 years. That's a long time when you consider that, according to recent research, 14 per cent of artificial tree buyers in the UK were planning to dump theirs after just one use.

Artificial Christmas trees are non-recyclable. An artificial tree will end up in landfill even if you have used it for ten years. Ocean Conservancy even found an artificial tree as part of their 2018 International Coastal Clean-up. If you no longer want your fake Christmas tree, see if you can donate it rather than send it to landfill.

So, if you do already have an artificial tree, keep using it for as long as possible. Or if you need to buy one, for example because of allergies, don't completely despair. There is always the option of buying a pre-loved artificial tree.

Real Trees

There is no doubt that a real tree can evoke feelings of nostalgia that you just don't get with an artificial tree. There's something magical about weaving your way through a maze of Christmas-smelling evergreens to choose your tree to take home. And it can be a lovely experience if you get yours from a local farm. Ours has hot chocolate tipis and sometimes even reindeer to see.

Real Christmas trees are a sustainable option with a much smaller carbon footprint than artificial ones. Especially when you choose a locally grown one. And depending on what you do with them after Christmas, they can even be carbon positive.

When buying a natural Christmas tree there is no need to worry about deforestation because the majority are grown as a horticultural crop and aren't felled from pre-existing forests. Real trees are a renewable resource, as at least one tree will be planted when one is harvested. At some plantations, they plant two or more new trees for every one harvested each year.

There are millions of Christmas trees growing in the UK at any one time, with all the benefits that trees give to the environment. Not only are they removing carbon from the atmosphere whilst they are growing, but they provide homes for local wildlife too. These trees would not be growing if it weren't for the Christmas tree market.

Your local Christmas tree farm will be happy to give you more details on how they grow their trees. But if you want to be reassured that your tree has been grown sustainably, and not in a way that's environmentally damaging, look for the FSC-certification logo. If you want a tree that's certified as organic and pesticide free, get one that's approved by the Soil Association.

The British Christmas Tree Growers Association website will show you where you can buy locally (www.bctga.co.uk).

Disposing of a real tree

Despite being wholly plant material, cut Christmas trees still need to be properly recycled. A natural Christmas tree left to decompose in landfill releases CO_2 and produces methane, a greenhouse gas that contributes to global warming. Burning or chipping your tree can reduce this carbon footprint by up to 80 per cent!

Most local authorities now offer a collection service for real trees that they shred to create chippings, which are then used in local parks and woodland areas. Or another option is to get crafty and use your tree branches and trunk for creating DIY decorations and coasters.

Pot-grown trees

If you are green-fingered, you could consider buying a potted Christmas tree with roots. With this option you can grow your tree outside and then reuse it again year after year. You can get your pot-grown Christmas tree in various sizes and although more costly to start with, it will cost you less in the long run. However, it will need some looking after and nurturing, of course, and you'll need a big enough pot and garden.

Rent a tree

Renting a living Christmas tree is becoming more popular and could give you the best of all worlds. It's got all the authentic festive joy you want, it's a sustainable option and there's little hassle, as it can be delivered to your door and then collected after Christmas is over. Lots of garden centres, plant nurseries and Christmas tree farms now offer the option to rent a tree. But apply the same discretion and make sure that it's grown sustainably by looking for either the FSC or Soil Association logo.

Some companies offer you the chance to name your tree and you might even be able to get the same one back the following year.

Make sure you stand your tree in a container that you can top up with water. Ideally try to top it up every day, as trees are thirsty. The average Christmas tree drinks up to 1–2 litres of water a day! And try to keep your tree in a cool, dry space, away from radiators or fires.

Alternatives to a Traditional Tree

Not everyone loves Christmas trees. If you are someone that finds them too much faff to put up, you don't have the space, or would like to take a totally different approach that is really eco-friendly, here are some alternative Christmas tree ideas you could try.

- If you already have a large indoor plant, just decorate it at Christmas time!

- Try a Christmas-lights tree, where you create a tree shape by securing fairy lights to a piece of plywood. This will create a glowing Christmas tree you can still gather around.

- You can easily repurpose leftover tomato cages from the summer and turn them into cute little Christmas trees to be used as either indoor or outdoor decorations.

- Book lovers can create a book tree. Once your books are piled high in the shape of a Christmas tree, just hang some foraged garlands from it, throw a star on top, and voila.

- Make a rustic birch branch Christmas tree. If you know someone with a birch tree in their garden, then you might not have to spend anything at all to make this one. The best time to prune a birch tree is early autumn so you will have to pre-plan. But once Christmas time comes around, simply place your branch in a pot, hang any ornaments you already have, and job done.

- For a recycled option, grab some cardboard and upcycle it into a Christmas tree. You could either cut out your tree shape and hang it on the wall or even create a 3D tree. Once you have the structure of your tree set up, you can make a fun project out of decorating it with everything from homemade ornaments to handwritten notes.

Decorations

I love to decorate my home with a natural and pared-back Scandi vibe at Christmas. Bringing nature indoors with plants and flowers is an easy but effective way to sustainably decorate. Why not add some house plants to your Christmas list?

My favourite decorations are eco-wreaths, hanging mistletoe and foraged greenery with a pop of colour in the berries. There are plenty of ideas for you in this chapter.

If you do prefer a full-on festive explosion, just make sure you look after your decorations with care. Avoid throwing unwanted decorations in the bin, and check out the best ways to donate instead.

Natural Decorations

Natural foraged materials are lovely to create with at Christmas time and a sustainable way to decorate. There's something special about the subtle scent of real pine and the deep red of berries – Mother Nature does it better than we ever could.

Decorating the table

- For the Christmas table, go all out and use armfuls of lush foraged foliage with some twinkling candles. Or go simple with a sprig on each plate.

- Gather up some holly, the iconic Christmas plant, and use it in your eco-wreath (see page 110) or in garlands for your mantlepiece, or lay sprigs around candles.

- Save pine cones. They make great decorations and can be used in your eco-wreath or wired into garlands. You could also pile a few in a bowl with fairy lights for a simple yet pretty effect.

- Hang mistletoe! Mistletoe has been a popular Christmas decoration since the 18th century. Its plump white berries and evergreen leaves are meant to symbolise fertility, which is why we kiss underneath it. Mistletoe grows wild on some trees as a parasite but if you don't manage to forage it, you can also buy some.

- Drape dried-orange garlands across the table or string across the window or fireplace as a simple and cost-effective way to decorate with a natural, minimalist vibe. (See page 83 for how to make a dried-orange garland.)

Decorating the tree

Tis the season for decorating gorgeous Christmas trees and I am all about making my Christmas tree personal and handmade. We have some ornaments that are older than me, which get lovingly unwrapped and rehung each year along with items the kids have made over the years. Our tree when it is decorated never fails to make me smile!

It has become the fashion to change the theme of your decorations year after year, which just isn't sustainable. So unless you're replacing broken pieces, try to reuse your decorations. If you do fancy a change, you could make your own or search in charity shops. If you are buying new then opt for ethically made. Places like Oxfam have some lovely unique handmade decorations.

A NOTE ON FAIRY LIGHTS

When a string of fairy lights breaks, often it's just one bulb or the fuse in the plug that needs replacing. If you can't fix them yourself, you might be lucky enough to have a repair café or shop near you. If you still have no luck, they can be recycled at your local recycling centre.

When you need to replace your fairy lights, swap to LEDs which are much more environmentally friendly than traditional bulbs. They use up to 80 per cent less energy so you'll help decrease your carbon footprint, and you'll save money, as they last up to 20 times longer than regular bulbs.

If every UK household swapped a string of incandescent lights for an LED equivalent, research suggests we could save more than 29,000 tonnes of CO_2 just over the 12 days of Christmas! And if you can't forego outdoor lighting, choose solar-powered lights. These are much better for the environment and local nocturnal wildlife than mains-powered ones.

Eco-wreath

A hedgerow-foraged Christmas wreath on an eco-friendly base looks lovely and will cost you hardly anything to make.

You can either begin with a ready-made wicker or wreath base (the easy option) or have a go at making your own – lots of local florists will offer wreath-making workshops in the run-up to Christmas.

YOU WILL NEED

Wreath base made from willow or wicker

Moss

Floristry wire or twine

Foliage: a mixture of greens, cones and berries

HOW TO MAKE

1   Start by padding one side of the wreath base with moss and wrapping around it with twine or floristry wire to secure it in place. Only cover the parts of the wreath base that you want to have foliage on; leave some of the willow or wicker showing, if you want.

2 The foliage you use for your wreath can be as simple or exotic as you like. Personally, I love the understated style of using Christmas tree trimmings, some berry springs and a little eucalyptus, but you can tailor yours to whatever you have around, adding extra embellishments if you like.

3 Bind the greenery and embellishments to the base using floristry wire or twine. To do this, poke the ends of your greenery into the moss a piece at a time and secure it by wrapping once or twice around the base with your wire or twine. It helps if your foliage all points the same way.

4 Loop some ribbon or twine around the top so that you can hang it up. After Christmas, keep hold of your wreath base, wire and twine to reuse the following year.

Popcorn Strings

Making popcorn strings is a fun activity to do with kids (or by yourself, if it's a quiet weekend in...). Don't expect perfection! It's more about the process and spending time together than the final product. There will be broken popcorn! You can easily pick up popcorn kernels from your local zero-waste shop or health food store. Hang your popcorn strings on your tree, decorate a window or hang them over your doors and fireplace.

Get popping!

YOU WILL NEED

Needle: if you are doing this with kids, the best needle to use is one that has a blunt tip and large eye, but is not much bigger than a regular sewing needle

Popcorn: this should be completely plain and slightly stale, so after popping leave it out for several hours, or even wait a day before stringing it

String: use twine or regular sewing thread doubled up and knotted once you have passed it through the eye of the needle

HOW TO MAKE

1 Thread your needle (with no more than 1 metre at a time to prevent the string tangling), double it up and tie a knot at the end.

2 Choose the fattest popcorn pieces for stringing and push the needle through the largest part.

3 Repeat until you have filled your section of string.

4 You can tie strings of popcorn together to make a longer one, if you wish.

Festive Foraging

Foraging is good for the soul, the planet and your pocket. I love heading off with my little basket and a pair of secateurs, my wellies and woolly hat on. It's a great activity to do on a lazy Sunday afternoon and kids enjoy it too, especially if there is the promise of eating blackberries (month dependant).

Here are some of my favourite craft projects to make your own Christmas decorations and gifts at home using materials you can easily gather from your garden or local hedgerows.

What to Forage

If you are new to foraging it can be a little daunting to know just where and what you can pick. There are some great apps (such as PlantNet Plant Identification, Forager's Buddy and Shroomify) that allow you to take images of the berries and leaves with guidance to help you identify them. The Woodland Trust also has plenty of information and some guides about seasonal foraging. Or you can join a local foraging guided walk, which is a brilliant way to discover new local areas.

The forager's code is to only take a little, making sure you are saving some for others, whilst respecting the wildlife and the environment. The most important thing is, if you can't identify it, don't pick it! And make sure that if you are on farmland, you have permission to be there.

Pine-Cone Firelighters

Pine-cone firelighters smell lovely and make a cute handmade present too. Just make sure the recipient has a fire to use them in!

If you are making them for yourself, they look gorgeous in a wooden or wicker bowl on the mantelpiece or next to the fireplace. When lighting the fire, throw in a couple of pine-cone firelighters with the kindling. As they burn, they will scent the room beautifully.

YOU WILL NEED

10 pine cones

2 cups soy or natural beeswax

10 drops essential oils (optional): this is really down to personal preference but I love a mix of cedarwood, frankincense and nutmeg to help create a lovely festive aroma

Tongs, if you have them

HOW TO MAKE

1 If the pine cones that you find are closed, they will open up inside in the warmth but may take a few days. To speed things up you can put them in a baking tray in the oven on its lowest setting. This takes 2–3 hours and will fill your kitchen with a lovely pine scent. Check on them every hour and give them a little move around.

2 Once the pine cones have opened, shake off any dirt or pine needles.

3 Heat your wax in a bain marie: place the wax in a heatproof bowl and set it over a pan of simmering water, making sure the bottom of the bowl doesn't touch the water. Or, if you have one, melt the wax in a double boiler.

4 If you want to add essential oils, this is the time to do it. The pine cones will smell lovely on their own though.

5 Once the wax has melted, remove it from the heat and allow to cool for a few moments – but not so long that it starts to solidify. You want the wax warm enough so that you can work with it, but not so hot that it burns your fingers, although you can use tongs if you prefer.

6 Dip the pine cones into the wax and gently swirl them so they are mostly covered. They should become immediately frosted with a white coating. If the wax goes on clear, it is not yet cool enough. If you have allowed it to cool too much, just warm it up briefly again.

7 Once you've covered each pine cone with wax, place them on wire rack or baking tray lined with baking paper to cool overnight (or for at least 2 hours).

Natural Napkin Rings

These simple foraged napkin rings are an unusual way to bring some nature to your Christmas dinner table. I like to use rosehip berries, gathered in the autumn. Cut the twigs in lengths and discard any leaves, then store in a cool, dark, dry place to prevent the hips from shrivelling. To help identify the rosehip berries and willow or hazel shoots, use an app on your phone or borrow a book from the library.

YOU WILL NEED

Willow or hazel shoots or twine

Pine sprigs

Rosehips (or other non-poisonous berries)

HOW TO MAKE

1   Gently bend the willow or hazel shoots into a small circle, wrapping the ends around each other. Make it just large enough for a napkin to fit through.

2   Weave in a few pine sprigs and rosehips (or other non-poisonous berries).

3   If you can't find any willow or hazel shoots, you could also wrap twine around your napkins to secure your foraged rosehips or pine sprigs.

Hedgerow Sloe Gin

Sloe gin is delicious and very easy to make! You will need to begin in the autumn, as it is best left in a cool, dark place for a few months before serving at Christmas time. One of the great things about sloe gin is that it improves over time, so you don't need to drink it all at once when it's open. You can serve your sloe gin neat, add it to your favourite tonic or even drizzle a little over ice cream. Make sloe royales by adding a drop to sparkling wine or champagne.

When I first started making sloe gin to give as a little gift at Christmas, I faced a very basic problem: I realised I had no idea where to actually find them. But if you look in any hedgerows you will most likely find a blackthorn bush, of which the sloes are the fruit, as they grow throughout most of the UK. Blackthorn bushes tend to be large and have oval-shaped leaves that are a lighter green than those of junipers. You can use an app or a book to help you identify the leaves. Sloe berries look a lot like dark blueberries with a pale coating, which can be wiped off with your thumb. Their long thorns can make harvesting a prickly business, so come prepared with gardening gloves.

The number of sloes you will find on a blackthorn each year will depend on the weather during the previous spring and summer. So some years you may be lucky and find loads of well-ripened sloes. Other years, particularly if it has been too wet and cold, you may have a harder job.

For the best flavour, wait until the berries are ripe before picking. They should be a rich dark purple and should squash easily between your fingertips. It's a good sign if they've already started to drop naturally to the ground.

If you're picking them for sloe gin, then traditionally you wait until after the first frosts. But there is no reason why you can't pick them earlier, bag them up and pop them in your freezer to mimic that first frost. The theory behind this is that the frost splits the skins so the juices can flow into your gin without you having to go to the effort of pricking all the berries.

For this hedgerow sloe gin you can add any foraged edibles that you like. Remember to check and if in doubt, don't add anything you aren't sure is edible.

YOU WILL NEED

2 handfuls of sloes

2 crab apples, chopped in half

A small handful of rosehips (or any mixture of edible hedgerow berries)

Sprig of rosemary

1 large sterilised glass jar or bottle (at least 1 litre) with a wide neck and a screw-on or airtight lid

Caster sugar – you will need to fill a third of your chosen container with sugar so measure this out first

1 litre bottle of gin (or vodka or whisky)

500ml glass bottle, if you are planning on decanting, or 100ml glass jars to make miniature gifts

Twine and gift tags, if making into gifts

HOW TO MAKE

1 Wash the sloes and seal them in an airtight bag. Freeze them overnight or until you're ready to make the gin.

2 Put your frozen sloes and other foraged edibles, including the rosemary, into your jar. You want it to be about a third full.

3 Add the sugar so the jar is about two-thirds full and then pour in the gin, leaving a 2cm gap at the top of the jar. Seal tightly and shake gently.

4 Store in a cool, dark place and swirl gently by rotating the jar every other day for a week. After the first week you only need to swirl it once a week for the next couple of months. After patiently waiting, your sloe gin should be dark red.

5 Before drinking, you will need to strain it. You can either do this each time you take a couple of measures by pouring the gin through a sieve into your glass and then putting any berries that come out back into the jar. Or strain it all into a smaller jar or bottle ready for using or giving as a gift.

6 To make your sloe gin into miniature gifts, pour into cute hexagonal or round 100ml mini glass jars.

7 Tie your jars with a piece of twine and a brown gift tag for a natural-looking gift. You could even write on the tag the name of your sloe gin in calligraphy or pretty lettering.

Being Together

One of my favourite things about Christmas is that people make more of an effort to spend time with each other. To help make your time with loved ones full of fun and enjoyment, try some of these simple, sustainable ideas.

An Evening In

Invite your friends round for a Christmas evening and spend some quality time together. Dress up and swap your gifts. You could each bring a different dish or a bottle of something. It's a great opportunity to play that Christmas playlist and serve some of your homemade Hedgerow Sloe Gin (see page 121)! For more ideas, check out the chapter on Low-waste Christmas Parties (see page 157).

Games Night

How about a festive games night? Each person can bring their favourite game with them, or you could play parlour games, like the two simple ones below, which don't require you to buy anything.

Heads Up! will provide hours of fun and laughter. Download the Heads Up! app and then hold your phone to your forehead while the room tries to describe, act out, sing or otherwise explain the word/s on the screen. There are endless categories to try.

If you don't want to use an app, write some ideas ahead of time onto Post-it notes to stick onto the guesser's forehead.

The Santa Hat Game involves getting everyone a Christmas hat, so raid the charity shops or ask everyone to bring their own. Before or when they arrive, pin the name of a Christmas character to the top of each one. Ask everyone to put on a hat without peeking at the name. Each person takes their turn asking questions to try to guess their identity. The winner is the first person to guess who he or she is.

Movie Night

Watching a movie at home can be just as fun as heading to your local cinema. Make an evening of it: put on your comfy PJs, make some popcorn, light the candles and then snuggle up together. You can do this as a family or invite your friends round for a Christmas-themed movie night with snacks and drinks. See how many Christmas movies you tick off the list this year. Here are our favourites:

- *The Santa Clause*
- *Miracle on 34th Street*
- *The Holiday*
- *Die Hard*
- *Gremlins*
- *Home Alone*
- *A Christmas Carol*
- *The Snowman*
- *Elf*
- *National Lampoon's Christmas Vacation*
- *The Christmas Chronicles*
- *A Muppet Family Christmas*

- *Scrooged*
- *The Polar Express*
- *It's a Wonderful Life*
- *A Christmas Story*
- *Christmas With The Kranks*
- *The Chronicles of Narnia*
- *Serendipity*
- *Little Women*
- *Bad Santa*
- *The Nightmare Before Christmas*
- *Mickey's Once Upon A Christmas*

Going Out

Santa's grotto. There's nothing more magical than visiting Santa Claus in his grotto. Check your local guides and listings to find the best ones near you. Keep your eyes peeled for ones that are free if you are trying to budget. Or find a grotto that incorporates a whole day out. Ever since the kids have been little we go to a farm where we make reindeer food, take part in a nativity with real animals, drink steamy hot chocolates and visit the real Santa. We look forward to it every year and it has now become one of our family traditions. All the family come and it's such a great Christmassy day.

Panto. If you want to see a panto but don't want to go to a big theatre, you could support a local amateur dramatics company. It's often a lot cheaper and a great way to give back to the community.

A wintery walk with a treat. Meet up with friends or go as a family for a winter walk. To make it more special, take a treat of hot chocolate in a thermos. You could even take some marshmallows if you want. Don't forget the mugs!

Look at the lights. If you have somewhere local that goes all out with the street decorations, make a night of it. I have friends who drive to their local lights and eat fish and chips in the car as a treat!

How to go carolling

Whether you go out and do it as a group, invite friends over for food and carols or go to church, research has shown that singing is good for you in many different ways – from keeping your lungs healthy, to helping you feel less alone. Singing songs you already know will make it less daunting and singing in a group means you don't need to worry too much about keeping in tune.

If you've ever fancied going out carolling but have no idea how or what to do, here are some tips.

- Find your group of carollers (you can ask friends and family or put out a note in your local community).

- Choose a few songs that you all know well enough to sing.

- It's a good idea to have a few practices together before you go out.

- Make sure you dress for the weather. Being cold and miserable won't make the experience much fun.

- Plan your route; try to stick to well-lit areas and bring a torch.

- Only ring the doorbell once and don't visit too late.

- Smile and have fun!

- If you are planning on collecting charity donations, make it clear with a label on a basket or bucket who you are collecting for, but don't make people feel under pressure to donate.

Cosy Pastimes

Christmas music. I tend to have the same Christmas album on repeat if I get the chance and not everyone likes it. So make a playlist together as a family or with a group of friends. Get each person to suggest a few of their favourites and they should all be happy!

Baking. This is a lovely calming activity. It's one for all the family and children will love getting their hands and your kitchen all messy (you might not love this bit so much, but just think of the delicious smells that will fill your kitchen). Then let the kids loose with icing and decorations and it will keep them entertained for a while. See page 43 for an easy recipe for Gingerbread Christmas Biscuits.

Or you could even get a group of friends together and have a Christmas bake-off!

Homemade gifts. Invite your friends and family round to make your homemade gifts together. Just be aware that if you end up gifting them what you make, it won't be a surprise! Check out the Creative Gifts chapter (page 41) for some ideas for what you could make.

Sharing books. A lovely way to spend some calm time together in the run-up to Christmas is with a bedtime Christmas story. If you've decided on having a Christmas book Advent (see the Alternative Advent Calendars chapter) then choose one a night to read together. You could even make an evening of it: grab your favourite Christmas stories and share them together with a hot chocolate before bed.

Sharing Christmas stories and reading aloud isn't just for kids. You could get together with friends or family and read some short stories or poems. Or maybe tell each other some funny family Christmas stories; I'm sure you will have plenty between you.

Christmas Dinner

Pigs in blankets, honey-glazed parsnips and chocolate oranges are just some of my favourite Christmas foods. Christmas is a time of year that's notoriously excessive when it comes to food and drink, and because of this we create a huge amount of waste.

In the UK, according to FoodCycle, we waste 5 million Christmas puddings, 2 million turkeys and 74 million mince pies every year. Considering how many people use food banks in this country, that's pretty sad. But with planning ahead, cooking smart and rethinking some old traditions, we can all make a difference and still enjoy a feast.

Planning Ahead

With a little planning you can avoid food waste as well as have a more pleasant and less stressful Christmas. Think through and plan all the meals – not just Christmas dinner, but the meals that you will have in the run-up to Christmas and in the days after. Plan in some meals that will use up leftovers and don't forget that shops are usually only shut for one day now, so don't overbuy!

The Christmas menu

The first thing to do is make a list of who is coming on the day. Then use that to work out how many people you're feeding for each meal, and whether you're going to be providing veggie, vegan or other options.

Decide what you are going to eat for the main meal, including the sides and dessert. If you are stuck when choosing what to cook, the Carbon Trust points out that turkey has a lower carbon footprint than beef, while vegetarian and vegan options have a lower carbon footprint still. If you are opting for red meat, make sure it's British. For turkey, try to buy organic and free-range from local farmers.

Once you know what you are having to eat, work out how much you will need. Don't forget to think about things like gravy too.

Only plan to serve things you know will get eaten. There is no point serving up a load of sprouts or cranberry sauce if only one person is going to eat them.

If you're unsure how many extra bits and pieces you might need, buy frozen, tinned or long-life foods that you can store and use up at a later date.

Think about the items on your list that you could make from scratch, to avoid non-recyclable packaging.

Buying ingredients

Plan out where you are going to buy your food. Maybe you already know suppliers who use minimal packaging. Could you get some of your food from a local refill shop? If you are ordering your shopping online, try to do it with one delivery from one place, rather than lots of different deliveries.

Buying the ingredients for your Christmas from local stores and markets will not only reduce your carbon footprint, but will also show your support for local businesses. Some other benefits to shopping local are:

- You will probably be using seasonal produce which means a lower carbon footprint as it won't have been transported from abroad.

- If you place an order with your local butcher, they will often let you pick up food in your own containers to save on waste.

- Local shops that make food on the premises will likely sell their produce in minimal packaging.

- Finding loose fruit and vegetables will be easier.

- Food is fresher if you're shopping at a local market, as it has come straight from the farmer and likely hasn't travelled a long distance to get there.

The edible garden

Winter is a time when your garden may look tired but there's still life in it. With a little bit of pre-planning, you can use whatever garden, allotment or window box that you have to grow your own decorative or edible plants for Christmas.

There is something so special about eating food you have grown from a seed. It always tastes better and is a great way to live more sustainably too!

Parsnips. Who doesn't have parsnips at Christmas? Last year we dug ours up from the allotment a few days before, so they were extra fresh! Parsnips are an easy-to-grow vegetable. They do take time, though, so need to be planted in April or May. In late October or early November, cover them with layers of straw to help protect them in cold weather. A few days before the big day, dig them up and store them in the refrigerator to build their sweetness. Any leftover parsnips make great soup!

Sage, bay, thyme and rosemary. These classic herbs can be grown at home in pots. They are easy to grow and are perfect to use in your own cooking or to gift to others, either as a plant or dried.

None of these herbs like wet roots, so grow them in pots that you can keep well drained and take care not to over-water them. You can grow sage from seed but the others are easier bought as plants or grown from cuttings.

Brussels sprouts. Sprouts are pretty much guaranteed on most Christmas tables. The perfect time to sow Brussels sprouts from seed is in March and April. But if you have missed the ideal planting time, by mid-summer you should still be able to buy young sprout plants that can then be planted out in their permanent positions. Space your plants 60cm apart in a sheltered and sunny spot. Water every 10 to 14 days, and watch them grow into tall spears of sprouts.

Vegetable Wellington

Serves 1

If you are debating ditching the traditional turkey this year, why not give a vegetarian or vegan Christmas dinner a go?

This vegetable wellington is just as good as turkey and local or homegrown vegetables will have the least carbon footprint of all your Christmas dinner options. Just make sure, if you are going vegetarian or vegan, that you check things like the stuffing and gravy too.

YOU WILL NEED

Your choice of vegetables: portobello mushrooms, peppers, courgettes, onions, beetroot, squash

Plain flour, for dusting

2 sheets of filo pastry

Balsamic reduction

Slices of vegan cheese (optional)

Olive oil

Salt and pepper

Cookie cutter or a food ring (about 8cm)

HOW TO MAKE

1 Using a food ring or cookie cutter, cut your vegetables into rings. Thinly slice the vegetables that can't be cut into rings to a similar size and thickness. You want to create a veggie stack that's about 5cm high.

2 In a frying pan over a medium-low heat, gently fry the vegetables in a little olive oil until they have softened, about 10 minutes. You may have to do this in batches.

3 Preheat your oven to 200°C/180°C fan/gas mark 6.

4 Dust your worktop lightly with flour and lay down a sheet of filo pastry. Brush this sheet with a little olive oil and lay the second sheet on top so they stick together.

5 Place the food ring/cookie cutter in the centre of the pastry sheets. Layer in your cooked vegetable rings to create a stack.

6 While doing this, season each layer with a little salt and pepper and drizzle over some balsamic reduction.

7 If you want to, you could add a slice of vegan cheese between the layers.

8 Carefully remove the food ring/cookie cutter and gather up the filo pastry around the stack of vegetables.

9 Pinch the filo together at the top to create a parcel, using a little water if needed.

10 Place horizontally on a baking sheet and bake in the oven for 12–14 minutes, or until golden brown.

11 Serve with your traditional roast potatoes and sides.

Leftovers

If you planned well then you shouldn't have too many leftovers. But if you do, they can be a versatile addition to your post-Christmas meals. You can create some delicious meals with minimal fuss.

Using up leftovers

- add leftover gravy to sauces for depth of flavour
- make a soup with leftover veggies
- add leftover meat or vegetables to an omelette or frittata
- create a fruit salad with leftover fruit
- add any leftovers to a stew
- cook a tasty turkey risotto with leftover turkey and vegetables

Storing leftovers

Store your leftovers carefully. Use reusable beeswax wraps instead of cling film and tinfoil to cut down on your waste. Or store in any airtight containers you have to hand.

Make sure your freezer is relatively empty before the festive season so that when you have leftovers that you know you won't eat straight away, you'll have room to store them. Remember to label them and add the date.

Boxing Day Bubble and Squeak

It can be challenging to use up leftover roast potatoes and sprouts after the Christmas Day feast, but here they get a delicious makeover. This recipe is really easy and makes a great addition to your Boxing Day brunch.

YOU WILL NEED

Leftover roast potatoes

Leftover Brussels sprouts, chopped

Pinch of dried chilli flakes (optional)

Cooked bacon, chopped (optional)

1 tablespoon cooking oil

Salt and pepper

HOW TO MAKE

1 Crush the roast potatoes with a masher or fork and mix with the chopped sprouts in a bowl. The starch in the potatoes will hold the mixture together.

2 Season well and, if you like, add a pinch of dried chilli flakes and/or chopped cooked bacon.

3 Mould the mixture into patties and put them to one side.

4 Heat the oil in a non-stick frying pan over a medium heat and then add the patties, cooking on each side for a few minutes until they are golden brown and warmed through.

Crackers

I do love a Christmas cracker but there is no doubt that the regular shop-bought versions are not particularly eco-friendly. The good news is that there are plenty of greener options for you. These will still provide masses of traditional fun but won't leave you with lots of waste and useless little plastic bits that just end up getting chucked.

Cracker Alternatives

Planning to give crackers a miss but still want something to liven up the table? You could introduce Christmas hats or headbands (that you keep and reuse), or even some festive activities. Some ideas could be:

- ★ Set up a Christmas pass the parcel, layered with jokes and riddles, with a zero-waste surprise in the middle.

- ★ Write down a challenge for each guest and place it under their plate. It could be a ridiculous phrase that they have to slip into the conversation or an odd action that they have to do during the meal (without laughing!).

- ★ Play the Christmas name game. Each person has a Christmas name – such as Santa or Rudolph – stuck to their forehead and they have to work out who they are by asking questions. You can only respond to each question with a yes or a no.

- ★ Create Christmas trivia questions. You could write one for each person to answer, or make them into a quiz and keep a score.

SOURCING ECO-FRIENDLY CRACKERS

If you feel like no Christmas table is complete without a bang, look for crackers that are British-made, recycled and recyclable, printed using vegetable-based inks, made with FSC paper and contain plastic-free gifts.

Reusable Crackers

One sustainable cracker option is to make your own, of course! The beauty of homemade Christmas crackers is that you can decide what to put in them. I keep ours simple with a hat, joke and a small surprise that will be used or eaten and not thrown away.

Make sure you keep all the parts so that you can put them back together next year.

IDEAS FOR FILLING THE CRACKERS

- Christmas hat made from paper or fabric

- Jokes or riddles – there are so many you can find online and you can go as classic or as cheesy as you like

- Something edible: sweets, chocolates or even a Gingerbread Christmas Biscuit (see page 43)

- A little packet of spice, with a simple recipe

- A packet of seeds

- A mini bottle of Hedgerow Sloe Gin (see page 121), or a mini glass jar with some cocoa powder and marshmallows, to make hot chocolate

- Other small items like useful stationery or toys that have been sourced second-hand (see the Pre-loved Gifts chapter on page 63 for ideas)

WHAT YOU'LL NEED

Cardboard tubes

Fabric or paper

Surprise items (see opposite)

Cracker snaps that are recyclable/ compostable (optional)

Washi tape

Ribbon or twine

HOW TO MAKE

1 Decide how many crackers you want to make (at least one per person) and save the inner cardboard tubes from rolls of toilet paper or kitchen roll. If you don't have these you can make cardboard inners for your crackers from cardboard boxes, pieces of card or even old Christmas cards.

2 Lay out your fabric and cut round your cardboard tubes so that you have enough length at either end to tie the fabric and leave an extra bit.

3 Next put your surprise items inside your cardboard inners, including the cracker snaps if you are using them. The cracker snaps will need to be taped to the inside of the cardboard and reachable from both ends.

4 Roll up the cardboard inners in the pieces of fabric to cover them. Secure the fabric in place with washi tape.

5 Tie the ends with either twine or ribbon, making sure that if you have used cracker snaps they are still reachable from both ends to pull. The cracker itself won't tear in half so decide who is going to win it beforehand. If you're not using cracker snaps, you could always shout BANG instead. Once all the crackers are pulled, untie the ends and open to reveal your surprises.

Shopping Green at Christmas

From shopping locally and purchasing handmade items to opting for organic or cruelty-free products, there are so many ways that you can make better choices at Christmas.

This is a great chance to take the time to find out what options there are locally. Do you have some unique shops or a refill market? Perhaps it could even kick-start a new way of shopping in the year ahead!

Buying Local

By shopping locally, you are helping the businesses in your community as well as cutting down on your carbon footprint. Not only has the distance you've travelled in person been minimised but if the item was made or grown locally then it has a smaller carbon footprint too.

Shopping locally in independent shops means you are more likely to be able to find a unique Christmas gift that isn't available anywhere else. Local shops often support local artists, food producers and growers, so you're buying products absolutely unique to your area, such as local honey. Independent bookshops often stock titles by local authors that might not be on the shelves of the major chains.

If your town doesn't have many shopping options, search for fairtrade or eco-friendly gifts online. Try to resist next-day delivery slots and opt for having multiple items delivered together or choosing a slot when the driver is already in the area.

Find a local refill market

If you have a local refill market, it's a great option for shopping greener. They tend to have a huge range of eco-friendly products – from spices and loose pasta to coffee beans and fresh peanut butter to bamboo toothbrushes. You can find some brilliant gifts!

Refill shops quite often have locally sourced items too. Locally roasted coffee beans and handmade soaps are two of my favourites.

In a refill shop you can choose the exact amount of an item you would like so there is less waste. You can also bring your own containers with you to take your items home in, which cuts down on plastic packaging, or most places will have a recycled selection there that you can use.

How to Avoid Greenwashing

Manufacturers and retailers sometimes tell you vague, unproven or even false claims about how eco-friendly their products are. This is called greenwashing and is meant to make you think products are green when they're not. For example, labels like 'chemical free' and 'non-toxic' are often meaningless.

The best way to determine whether a product is eco-friendly is to rely on third-party certification. Look for products with labels from reliable organisations. For example:

- **Fairtrade:** fairtrade offers farmers and workers in developing countries a better deal, so choosing fairtrade gives you the opportunity to improve workers' lives and invest in their future.

- **Leaping Bunny:** not only will the companies with the Leaping Bunny certificate be completely free from animal testing, their suppliers will also be cruelty-free, so you end up with a product that is 100 per cent free from animal testing.

- **Global Organic Textile Standard (GOTS):** the GOTS certificate ensures the organic status of textiles, from the harvesting of the raw materials to environmentally and socially responsible manufacturing to labelling.

- **Soil Association Organic Standard:** organic certification for farmers, growers, food processors and packers, retailers, caterers, textile producers, health and beauty manufacturers and importers in the UK and internationally.

Low-waste Christmas Parties

Christmas is a great time to socialise and as the cold nights draw in, it's fun to get dressed up in sparkles and get into the festive spirit.

With a few small changes, you can easily make your Christmas parties low-waste. For example, doing the catering yourself means that you don't need to buy plastic-wrapped convenience food. Plus it usually works out less expensive, and you can make it look nicer too! Don't worry, you don't need to be an expert cook for the recipes in this section. I've got you covered.

How to Have a Green Party

Have fun with the theme

When you invite your guests, you could tell them you have a sustainable dress code. If you're having a Christmas jumper party, make the rules fun. Tell your guests that their Christmas jumper must be second-hand, recycled, a hand-me-down, one they already own from a previous year or one they have created themselves with upcycled home items.

Don't send out physical invitations

Keep your invitations virtual. If you can't ask your friends to your party in person, create a Facebook event or send an email. Or you could get fancy and create an invite using an online platform. These tend to charge a small fee, but when the recipient accepts your invitation, it immediately saves the event in their phone.

Use the decorations you already have

Your house will already be dressed up for Christmas, so make the most of it. Bring more nature inside if you need to and add natural candles and LED fairy lights to help create that Christmas atmosphere.

If you are holding your party somewhere else, take your Christmas decorations from home or look for local hire companies. Think about using decorations that can be reused rather than purchasing single-use decorations. For example, you can check your local second-hand store for vintage linens rather than disposable tablecloths and napkins.

Do away with disposable cups and plates

The most obvious way to cut down on party waste, of course, is by ditching the disposable plates, cups and cutlery. They aren't very good anyway!

Instead, use the real stuff, which is what you probably already have at home. Yes, they can be breakable but just don't put your best china out. And if there aren't enough sets for everyone:

- Look for local hire companies
- Ask local friends and family
- Source items in second-hand shops or on local selling sites/pages

My personal preference is a collection of vintage china plates with mismatched patterns. Not only is it cute but if one breaks you don't have to buy another to make up a matching set. And as they aren't Christmas themed you can use them for parties throughout the year.

If you don't normally need all of these party supplies and you don't have space in your cupboards for them, pack them up into a box to store somewhere. You can also then lend your box out to friends and family for their events too.

Cleaning up

Cleaning up is unfortunately a part of every party and it is no different at Christmas. You shouldn't have much waste after following these ideas, but make sure your guests know where your recycling bins are.

A food compost bin is great for vegetable peelings and coffee grounds. Any edible leftovers should never go straight in the bin. You can instead encourage your guests to take home some of the leftover food and drinks, or share with your neighbours and colleagues at work! Still more leftovers? Take them to a food bank.

Think about the cleaning products that you use too. (Check out the Eco-friendly Cleaning chapter on page 183.)

You can also apply these ideas to your office Christmas party. Have everyone bring in a plate of homemade food rather than anything pre-packaged and keep disposable drinks to a minimum, opting for those that can be recycled.

Christmas Tree Focaccia   Serves 8

This tear-apart Christmas tree focaccia will be a real crowd-pleaser. Baking your own canapés means you can give your guests something to snack on without resorting to pre-made versions that come in lots of plastic wrapping.

It will look great so remember to take a photo before serving – it won't last long! This Christmas tree focaccia is best served warm so put it into the oven when your guests are due to start arriving.

YOU WILL NEED:

500g strong white bread flour, plus extra for dusting (organic if possible)

½ tablespoon fast-action yeast

300ml water at room temperature

3 tablespoons butter, or a dairy-free alternative

6 garlic cloves, crushed

A large handful of parsley, to garnish (optional)

A handful of grated Parmesan cheese or mozzarella cheese, to garnish (optional)

Olive oil

Salt

HOW TO MAKE

1 Place the flour, yeast and a pinch of salt in a large mixing bowl. Stir to combine. Make a well in the middle, then add 3 tablespoons of olive oil and the water. Mix with a wooden spoon until it comes together and starts to resemble a dough.

2 Flour your surface before tipping out your dough and kneading for roughly 5 minutes. Add more flour if it is still really sticky.

3 Place the dough in a bowl and cover with a tea towel to prove for 1 hour, or until the dough has doubled in size.

4 Once your dough has doubled in size, flour your surface again. Tear off a small piece of dough and roll it into a ball (roughly the size of a golf ball). Repeat with the remaining dough.

5 Place your first ball at the top of a large baking tray lined with baking paper, in the middle. Then place two dough balls beneath the first, then three, and so on, to make a tree shape.

6 Cover your dough ball Christmas tree with the tea towel and leave it to prove for a further 20 minutes.

7 Preheat the oven to 220°C/200°C fan/gas mark 7.

8 Melt the butter with 1 tablespoon of olive oil in a small pan on a medium heat. Add the crushed garlic and cook for 2 minutes.

9 Brush the focaccia with half of the garlic oil, then bake it in the oven for 15 minutes, or until golden brown.

10 When your Christmas tree focaccia is cooked, remove it from the oven and transfer it to a serving plate or board. Brush it again with the garlic oil.

11 Garnish with chopped parsley, grated Parmesan or mozzarella and/or a generous sprinkling of salt, if you like.

Easy Vegan Cheesecake

This delicious vegan chocolate cheesecake is quick and easy to make, and being homemade it's a more eco-friendly dessert for your guests. The cheesecake will last for five days in the fridge, so it's a great one to make in advance.

YOU WILL NEED:

2–3 tablespoons butter substitute

1 pack of chocolate Bourbons

1 tin of coconut milk, chilled

200g dark chocolate

2 tablespoons icing sugar

1 tablespoon vanilla essence

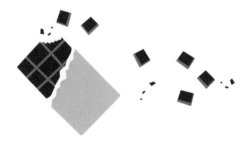

HOW TO MAKE

1 Grease a round cake tin (20–24cm) with some of your butter substitute.

2 To make the base, blitz the Bourbon biscuits in a food processor until crumbly, then tip into a large mixing bowl along with the rest of the butter substitute. Mix with a spoon until it sticks together. Press your biscuit base evenly into the lined cake tin.

3 Pour the chilled tin of coconut milk into a bowl and whisk with a balloon whisk until bubbly.

4 Melt the chocolate in the microwave in 10-second bursts, stirring each time. Or use a bain marie: place the chocolate in a heatproof bowl and sit the bowl over a pan of barely simmering water, making sure the bottom of the bowl doesn't touch the water. Allow the chocolate to melt, stirring occasionally.

5 Once the chocolate has melted, add it to the coconut milk.

6 Sift in the icing sugar and add the vanilla essence. Whisk your mixture until it has thickened and forms peaks. Pour into the cake tin and place the tin in the fridge for a few hours to set before serving.

Mulled Wine   Serves 8

Love it or hate it, mulled wine is wonderfully festive. I'm always lured in by its Christmassy aroma and will choose it over a G&T every time. This recipe isn't too tricky and you can change up the flavourings to really make it your own.

Warming up a large batch of this mulled wine will give the house a lovely smell and will discourage people from drinking disposable drinks. I have included an alcoholic and non-alcoholic option so that no one is left out.

YOU WILL NEED:

2 unwaxed oranges

The peel from 1 lemon

150g caster sugar or soft brown sugar (use a bit less if you don't want it as sweet!)

4 cloves

2 vanilla pods

1 cinnamon stick

A pinch of freshly grated nutmeg

A pinch of ginger (grated fresh or ground)

2 bottles of fruity organic red wine OR, for a non-alcoholic version, 750ml pomegranate or cranberry juice and 500ml apple juice

HOW TO MAKE

1 Peel and juice 1 orange then place the orange juice, orange peel, lemon peel, sugar and spices in a large saucepan.

2 Pour in enough wine, or pomegranate or cranberry juice, so that the sugar is just covered and heat gently until the sugar has dissolved, stirring occasionally. Bring to the boil and cook for 5–8 minutes until you have a thick syrup.

3 Meanwhile, cut your remaining orange into slices to use as a garnish. If you aren't serving your mulled wine immediately, this can be done later.

4 Turn the heat down and pour the rest of the wine or juice into the saucepan and give it a stir. Gently heat for around 5 minutes.

5 When it's warm and delicious it is ready to be served in heatproof glasses.

Festive Outfits

Christmas tends to encourage us to buy lots of new clothes. A new Christmas jumper, new matching Christmas-themed family PJs, a fabulous new sparkly outfit for a Christmas party...and that's before we've even decided what to wear on Christmas Day and New Year's Eve! However, there are plenty of ways we can have that perfect Christmas wardrobe but in a more sustainable way.

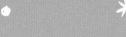

Customise a Christmas Jumper

Christmas jumpers tend to be worn once or twice before being discarded. But as one of the main culprits for creating Christmas clothing waste, we really need to think of a Christmas jumper as being for life and not just for Christmas.

If you are feeling crafty then why not customise an old jumper or cardigan instead of buying something new?

* Use leftover yarn to sew on snowflakes, holly leaves or trees. You will be able to find templates online.

* Make yourself a Christmassy paper chain and wear it around your neck over the top of a plain or sparkly jumper you already have.

* Sew on Christmas-coloured pompoms made from felt or wool.

* Source some second-hand baubles to sew on.

Swapping Not Shopping

If you swap party clothing, you can have something new to wear each time without having to buy anything. Of course, this does rely on you having friends and family who are a similar size to you!

The fast-fashion industry that creates high-street clothing is a huge problem for the planet. The process of making new clothes uses up vital resources such as water and releases dangerous chemicals into the environment.

Swapping clothes prevents perfectly usable and lovely items from unnecessarily ending up in our overflowing landfills. By swapping instead of shopping, you help to keep items of clothing in use for longer. According to research by WRAP, extending the useful life of your clothing by nine months reduces its carbon, water and waste footprints by around 20% each.

Swapping is also really good fun!

Clothing swish

A clothing swish is where a group of people bring at least one item of clothing that they no longer want and everyone swaps. Bring along the clothes you want to trade and you'll be given one token per item. Make sure they are good quality, otherwise they won't be accepted. It's a great way to get yourself some new items of clothing without buying new. You could arrange a Christmas swish full of Christmas jumpers and Christmas outfits. I would definitely go to one of those! In fact, it's particularly beneficial for Christmas items, as these tend to only get worn once or twice.

Pre-loved Clothing

I love clothes, I always have done and I always will. But I realised a few years ago I had a real problem with fast fashion. After burying my head in the sand for too long I decided to put myself on what turned out to be a year-long ban on buying any new clothes. During this year I learned a lot about shopping for second-hand clothes, and it's still my go-to, whether for me or the kids. Not only have I saved loads of money, I also have a wardrobe full of better-quality clothes. I can also confirm that none of my second-hand and vintage clothes smell old!

There are so many benefits of buying pre-loved fashion. Here are some of them:

- You save money on items that would cost more new
- You are reducing the demand for cheap and unethical labour
- You reduce the quantity of clothes going to landfill
- You help to extend the life cycle of fashion items
- You are helping to lower the creation of carbon emissions by not buying new clothes
- Charity shops benefit from your money
- You can, with a little searching, discover high-end fashion pieces or high-quality items at an affordable price

Where to shop

If you are looking for something specific like Christmas jumpers, start looking in November. Most Christmas jumpers sold in charity shops and online have only been worn once, at the most a handful of times, so you will end up getting an item that is pretty much brand new. The same goes for Christmas-themed outfits and sparkly dresses.

There are so many places to look when buying pre-loved and vintage fashion. Not only do you have your local charity shops, but all of these are accessible online: ASOS Vintage, Beyond Retro, Depop, Ebay, Etsy, Farfetch, Oxfam's online shop, Rokit Vintage, Vestiaire Collective and Vinted. Many charity shops are now turning to online selling too.

If you have more than one child, keep your Christmas jumpers to pass on to the next one or swap with friends. The same goes with any other Christmas outfits, and if you opt for a Scandi or Fair Isle-style Christmas jumper, you can wear it all winter long.

See page 155 for tips on How to Avoid Greenwashing.

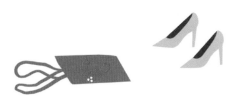

Sustainable Beauty

This time two years ago our shower and bathroom surfaces were littered with bottle upon bottle of plastic-packaged products that I very rarely used. Random bottles of gifted shower gel were shoved to the back of our overflowing cupboard. The clutter was totally overwhelming and I could never find what I was looking for. Sound familiar?

I gradually reduced the number of products and started to slowly replace those that I did use with ones in plastic-free packaging or, even better, with zero-waste products made from natural ingredients and that are cruelty-free. Now my bathroom is calmer and my skin is better – a huge bonus! Here are some of my top tips.

Sustainable Bathroom Swaps

Christmas is a time of year when you are likely to spend a little more time on your appearance, maybe buying a new lipstick, aftershave or some bathroom products for relaxing over the holidays. So don't add to the plastic clutter when you are buying anything new. There are lots of better alternatives out there.

- Swap your bottle of shampoo and conditioner for a bar. There are so many to choose from. You can also get both as a liquid made from natural ingredients and in sustainable packaging.

- Instead of bubble bath in a plastic bottle, buy a bubble bar or natural bath oils, or have a go at making your own bath soak (see page 181).

- Swap disposable face wipes for reusable face wipes. I have a mixture of crochet and bamboo rounds. I store them in a glass jar and then when I have used them, I put them in a little string bag that I wash with the towels. You can buy sets of these or have a go at crocheting your own to gift in a bundle with some natural face cleanser.

- Change to a bamboo toothbrush or eco toothbrush heads, natural toothpaste and eco dental floss. They are just as good!

- Treat yourself to a safety razor. I love using a safety razor. Am I slightly scared of it? Yes. But only a little. I've used one for over a year now and with a little care and going slow, I haven't had any problems.

- Try a bar of handmade soap made from natural ingredients instead of your usual shower gel. I've found that these leave even my sensitive skin feeling nice and moisturised. If you really can't give up your shower gel, there are plenty of natural, cruelty-free products available. Some come in refillable bottles or even glass.

- Change your bottles of handwash for a bar of soap. We use coconut, coir or bamboo soap dishes too, so they don't go all soggy. You could gift a nice handmade soap and soap dish together.

- Cruelty-free make-up is becoming easier to find. A lot now make their products in more sustainable packaging too. You will be surprised at the range out there.

- Opt for organic facial oils and creams, made with natural ingredients, from small independent companies. I have found some great products that have really improved my skin.

Pine-Scented Bath Soak

This bath soak makes a lovely gift, but make sure you save some for yourself too. Candlelit baths around Christmas time can be a great way to relax and have some downtime in what can be a hectic month.

You can make this in different quantities, just make sure you have the same ratio of ingredients.

To give this as a gift, attach a muslin bag to the jar along with some instructions.

YOU WILL NEED

1 cup oats (rolled or instant, as both will work)

1 cup Epsom salts

A small handful of pine needles, chopped (you can use other dried flower petals if you prefer, or lavender)

Glass jar with lid

Muslin drawstring bag

HOW TO MAKE

1 Place the oats, Epsom salts and pine needles in a glass jar. You want an equal amount of oats and salts.

2 Screw the lid on tightly.

3 To use, add 2 tablespoons of the mixture to your muslin bag and place the bag in your bath whilst it is running.

Eco-friendly Cleaning

There's no escaping cleaning, even at Christmas time! Whether you are cleaning up in preparation for Christmas, after Christmas parties or after Christmas Day, there will be cleaning to do. But you can easily make it greener.

Homemade Cleaning Products

For a long time, I didn't question the need for chemicals in the cleaning products I bought. They seemed like the only option to make sure everything was actually clean and germ free.

However, many shop-bought cleaning products contain really harsh chemicals that are dangerous if ingested, touched or even breathed in. Not only are the chemicals in them potentially dangerous to us, they can end up in our waterways, damaging wildlife and the environment. And then there's the fact that most store-bought cleaning products are packaged in plastic throwaway bottles. Once you start to think about it, it's completely contradictory to be using potentially hazardous products to try to make our homes safer.

It's not just the seemingly endless array of cleaning products on the market that can cause problems. Many of the items we use to clean – from washing-up sponges to window squeegees – are made out of and packaged in non-recyclable materials. I changed to eco cleaning products first and then decided to have a go at making my own. It's really quick and easy, it works out cheaper, it's better for the environment and better for us.

With three natural cleaners – baking soda, white vinegar and lemon juice – you can clean your home without any chemicals!

Lemons

⭐ Lemons have antiseptic and antibacterial properties and are a natural deodoriser.

⭐ Rub a slice of lemon over a chopping block to reduce bacteria.

⭐ Mix a bit of lemon juice with baking soda to remove stains from plastic containers.

⭐ Add half a lemon to your kettle and then boil it to remove limescale.

⭐ To clean your microwave, squeeze the juice of a lemon into a microwavable bowl and cook for 3 minutes. Leave it to stand for another 5 minutes, but do not open the door. Then wipe the inside of the microwave with a clean, dry rag.

Baking soda

Baking soda cleans and deodorises, softens water and scours.

⭐ You can easily absorb any lingering strong odours by placing 1 cup of baking soda in the fridge. You can also get rid of any bin stinks by placing some baking soda at the bottom of your rubbish bins.

⭐ For carpet odours, combine 10–20 drops of your favourite essential oil with 1 cup of baking soda and sprinkle liberally on the carpet. Allow to sit for a few hours before vacuuming.

⭐ To clean your toilet, add 1 cup of baking soda to the toilet bowl, then add 1 to 2 cups of vinegar, which will create a fizzing action. Let the solution sit for 10 minutes. Use a toilet brush to swish the solution around the bowl, making sure to get the solution onto any stains that are above the water line. Then flush away!

White vinegar

White vinegar, not to be confused with malt vinegar, cuts grease and removes mildew, odours and some stains.

- Use vinegar to remove grime and mineral build-up on your showerhead. Either use a small plastic container with enough vinegar to soak the showerhead, or alternatively spray it on. Leave it overnight and you'll see the nasty build-up and grime has dissolved the next day. Then just turn the shower on to rinse clean.

- To remove wine stains (from cotton or polycotton fabrics), sponge them directly with white vinegar – just make sure you do this within 24 hours.

- After the stains disappear, wash them according to their care label and you're done.

- White vinegar will also dissolve any kids' play slime you find on fabric sofas or carpets. You're welcome!

DIY All-Purpose Cleaner

This DIY homemade all-purpose cleaner is not only safe and made from natural ingredients (it only contains four ingredients, one of which is water!), but it's really effective. Use it on kitchen and bathroom surfaces, cabinets, the inside of the fridge/freezer and some appliances. It makes metal really shiny! However, don't use it on granite or marble countertops – the natural stone can be etched by the vinegar.

The Christmas-scented essential oils will mask the smell of vinegar; if any remains, it goes away after a minute of using. Use this spray with either shop-bought reusable cleaning cloths or make your own from old clothing or fabric. If you don't want a Christmas scent, lemon, orange and tea tree oil work well, with tea tree also possessing natural antibacterial properties.

YOU WILL NEED

½ cup distilled white vinegar

5 drops of orange essential oil and 5 drops of cinnamon essential oil, or the peel of 1 orange and 2 cinnamon sticks

2 cups hot water

A purpose-bought glass bottle with a spray top that you can keep reusing (you can find these in most zero-waste shops) or reuse a cleaned-out plastic spray bottle

HOW TO MAKE

1 Pour the vinegar into your glass bottle.

2 Add the essential oils or orange peel and cinnamon sticks.

3 Top it up with hot water.

4 Fit the bottle with the spray top, then gently swirl it to mix everything together.

5 Use immediately or as needed. It doesn't have a use-by date.

Giving Back

You can spread some love and positivity at Christmas time by getting involved in your local community – making it a nicer, greener and friendlier place to live.

How to Get Involved

Supporting your local community can help you to feel part of
something and to gain a sense of togetherness. If you tend to feel
lonely at Christmas, or if you aren't particularly looking forward
to Christmas this year, getting involved can help you to feel more
positive and give you a sense of purpose.

These ideas are by no means exhaustive but will give you a good starting point if you are wondering what you can do to get involved.

- ✦ Join in with or start **a collection within your community to create Christmas hampers** for those in need or those who would benefit from a pick-me-up in your local community.

- ✦ **Volunteer.** There will be so many organisations looking for extra volunteers in the run-up to Christmas. Food banks, soup kitchens, animal shelters and many more. You may even decide to keep this up into the new year.

- ✦ **Create a reverse Advent**. A reverse Advent calendar is a great way to get younger family members to understand that some people aren't as fortunate. See the Reverse Advent Calendar section on page 22. Donate to local families in need or a local food bank. (You don't need to do 24 items, even 1 tin helps.)

- ✦ **Offer a seat at the table this Christmas**. If you can do this, it is such a lovely idea. Maybe you know someone locally who will otherwise be spending Christmas Day on their own. Perhaps they are recently widowed and have no nearby family or it's your friend's first Christmas in a split family without the kids for the day. You could make a huge difference to someone's Christmas.

- ✦ **Offer a spare room.** If you wanted to go one step further you could offer a spare room for someone in need over the Christmas period.

- ✦ **Organise a local Christmas litter pick**.

- Do some **random acts of kindness.** Simple unexpected acts of kindness at Christmas can really brighten someone's day and make you feel good as well. You could pay for the person's coffee behind you in the coffee line, leave a bunch of foraged Christmas greenery on a local doorstep or donate old towels and blankets to an animal shelter.

- **Offer a taxi service for elderly people** in your community who are unable to transport themselves on Christmas day.

- See if your local care home is having a **carolling evening** and go along. Take the kids too!

- **Share a Christmas story** with someone who doesn't have family who visit. You can ask at local care homes or sheltered housing.

- See if there are any local **Christmas events for the elderly** in your community that you can help with, or create your own.

- Animals are often forgotten about when we think of volunteering at Christmas time, but **local animal shelters** will always be grateful for any support. And if you are thinking of getting a pet, always try to rehome first.

New Traditions

At the beginning of this book, I talked about how to make Christmas your own. If you look back at the exercise you did on page 3 to describe your perfect Christmas, is there anything you would change about it now?

I would recommend revisiting this exercise each year. As your celebration evolves into one that is greener and more personal, your version of the best Christmas will grow and change too.

What Are Your New Traditions?

As you spend less time wading through that big pile of presents and rushing from one thing to another, you will allow yourself the time to slow down and enjoy the simple moments. With more planning and less stuff, you will be able to introduce some new, greener traditions that you can all look forward to each year, that you pass on to your children and they hopefully pass on to theirs. Traditions like:

- Foraging together for Christmas decorations
- Planning and making your homemade gifts
- Sharing a book together each night as part of your book Advent
- Picking your real Christmas tree from a local farm
- Drinking hot chocolate from a flask on a wintery walk
- Singing carols together
- Volunteering and giving back to the community
- Cooking up an amazing turkey risotto with leftovers
- Pulling your own homemade crackers and laughing at the rubbish jokes
- Opening your reusable Advent calendar with excitement to see what you will be doing that day
- Finding the perfect pre-loved gift for someone

Living a greener life is a journey not a destination. Every little change that you make will help the planet. And so, as you start to experience the joy that a green Christmas can bring, try to spread the good word about what we can all do to have a sustainable and happy festive season.

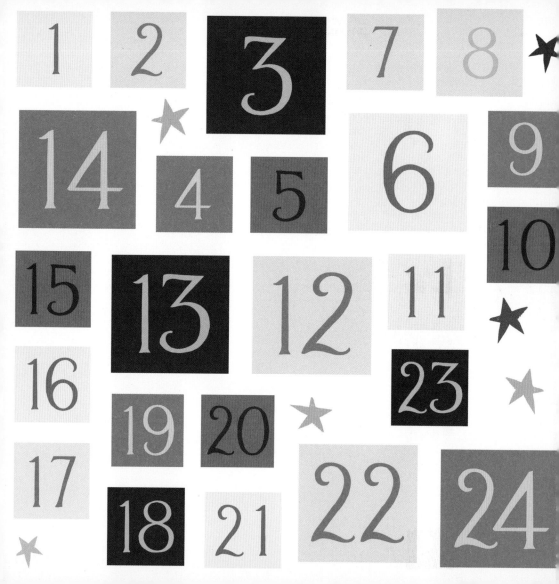